WHO

SHALL

BE GOD?

a selection

of sermons

WHO

SHALL

BE GOD?

a selection

of sermons

ALVIN N.
ROGNESS

augsburg

publishing

house

minneapolis

minnesota

Printed and manufactured in the United States of America
by Augsburg Publishing House, Minneapolis, Minnesota

CONTENTS

The King Meek

> *Rejoice greatly, O daughter of Zion; shout, O daughter of Jerusalem: behold, thy King cometh unto thee: he is just, and having salvation; lowly, and riding upon an ass, and upon a colt the foal of an ass.* ZECHARIAH 9:9

He came meek.

Have you ever thought how things might have been if Christ had not come lowly as a babe in Bethlehem's stable, or meek as a commonplace preacher on a donkey, or unresisting as a sacrifice on Calvary's cross? He would not have had to come in such complete humility. He could have chosen a blazing pathway through the skies, flanked by millions of armored angels. He could have circled the earth with the thunder of a thousand tornadoes and typhoons, and with a fireworks display of bursting planets and stars. He could have established His throne on the peaks of the Himalayas or the Swiss Alps, and ever after policed every household with secret cherubim and seraphim. He could have brought

1

to swift and unrelenting justice any budding
Nebuchadnezzar or Nero or Stalin. And He could
have won the paralyzing obedience of every
trembling child of men.

Why did the Almighty God, the King of kings,
the Sovereign Judge of heaven and earth choose to
invade the earth in such bewildering quietness?

It is not for us to make a brief for God. His
ways need not pass inspection before the feeble
minds of men. But this much seems certain, that
the sort of response He would have elicited from
you and me by an explosive display of His power
was not the sort of response He wanted.

He could have won our *fear*. But He was playing for bigger stakes. He had set out to win our
love, and with love our freedom. Fear always
imprisons, paralyzes and drives a person into the
narrow cell of extreme self-concern. Love, on the
other hand, casts out fear, sets a person free, and
gives him feet and wings to escape the prison
walls of self-anxiety, self-defence and self-pity.
God had created us to be sons in His Kingdom,
comrades of God and the angels in this business
of managing and enjoying the universe. Could
He, the great God, be a bungler, and for the
small and immediate prize of enforced obedience,
crush the spirit of man into the cowering slavery
of fear? Better to lose him altogether than
to win man on any other terms than love and
freedom!

Tagore in his little volume, *Fireflies,* says, "The clumsiness of power spoils the key and uses the pickaxe." And God is not clumsy. He chose to use the key of infinite love and suffering and not the pickaxe of power. It is said that Stalin had the fanatical homage of hundreds of millions, but if that is so it is equally true that mixed with this adoration was the fear and dread of the very power that breeds adoration. It is the demonic servitude of man become animal, and not of man raised to divine and unfettered freedom. God is no celestial tyrant coveting the homage of millions of dogs wagging their tails. He desires the free love of men who have become sons in His household. It was therefore that He elected to come not with power, but in lowliness and humility.

Moreover, how could He have taught man the deep lesson of suffering had He Himself not come as a suffering Servant? It is better to suffer than to cause suffering. Out of first century Rome two names have lived. One is Nero, the emperor who in the mania of power murdered his son and his wife and who is credited with burning Rome for a poetic whim. The other is Paul whose life of buffetings and sufferings ended in Roman martyrdom. History's appraisal of the two men and their manner of life is epitomized in the fact that today we name our sons Paul and our dogs Nero. In fair tribute to our dogs, we ought perhaps give them also a better name. There is untold strength and nobility in the patient love which suffers pain and injustice; there is only shame and personal disintegration in the brute power which causes pain and injustice.

At best it is difficult for men to learn this lesson. If God Himself should have failed to reveal in His own Person this profound truth of His Kingdom, how would men ever have learned it? The disciples themselves wrangled for positions of power in the Kingdom, and Christ found it necessary again and again to remind them of the noble character of service and suffering. And down through the centuries it has always been the witness of selfless service and voluntary suffering which has ennobled the Christian man and community.

It took none less than the Great King Himself, "who for the joy that was set before Him endured the cross, despising the shame," to teach us the sublime lesson of suffering. He had taken into His all-embracing heart the sins of all men and made them His own. His disciples had seen Him interrupt any task to ease the pain and anguish of the most wretched of human beings. They had seen Him weep at the graveside of a friend. They had watched Him endure without bitterness the base injustices of Good Friday. It was little wonder that when the resurrection opened their eyes to the fact that He was the incarnate God the strange nobility of suffering should become a flaming and transforming mode of life for them. That which shook the ancient world was not the spectacle of their power but the witness of their suffering. They, too, had learned that for the joy that was set before them, they could endure a cross and care nothing for its shame.

But there was a third, and more important, reason for Christ taking the form of a man, a suffering servant. Quite apart from any response He might arouse in man and quite apart from any padagogical value His life might have, He had entered this fallen world to redeem it. He had entered this battlefield of flesh and blood to do war against a foe and win. He had entered the court-room of man's trial to pay the penalty for man's sins with His suffering and death. His incarnation was not primarily an encounter between God and man; it was God coming to grips with man's foe, the devil.

Let us not forget that He came explicitly to suffer and to die. And let us not forget that Satan tried to keep Him from suffering and dying. Three times in the desert Satan had tried to make Him change His mind. It was as if Satan pleaded with Him, "Be an uncle-provider if you must, and change stones into bread for the human race; be a miracle-man if you desire, and win their awe by casting yourself down from the pinnacle of the temple; be a ruler with might, and let the children of men grovel before your power— but do not be a suffering and dying savior." Nor did Satan cease his persuasions. Through the voice of Peter he tried to dissuade Jesus from going to the Jerusalem passover; in the voices of the Palm Sunday multitude he tried to entice Him with the prospect of David's ancient rule; in the raucous cries of the Golgotha rabble he jeered Him to come down from the cross. Satan knew, and Jesus knew, that if He could be kept from dying Satan would have won the encounter and the world would have been left unredeemed. But Jesus was not driven nor beguiled off the field. He drove on into Satan's last stronghold, death; and with Christ's dying the stronghold itself fell. Death was overcome.

When the young shepherd boy, David, faced Goliath, the Israelites were arrayed on one side and the Philistines on the other. Both sides waited with bated breath the outcome. For, if Goliath had won, Israel would be slaves to the enemy. If David won they would be freemen and victors, and their enemies their slaves.

Little did the human race realize that at Golgotha's cross their eternal fate or destiny hung in the balance. This was the eternal duel for the salvation of men. In Christ's victory they became victors. With Christ's death they were made free from the guilt, punishment and dominion of sin.

He had become their mighty Brother who for them and in their stead had fulfilled the law and won the victory. Henceforth, placing their trust in Him they became heirs of the eternal kingdom.

When in 1945 the Allies overcame the Nazi powers in central Europe, the people of Norway and Denmark, unarmed and in bondage, suddenly became freemen again. The victory of another, hundreds of miles away, did not make them vassals of the conquering nations; it set them free.

In faith, we are to rise up as freemen in Christ. We are free of the guilt of past sins; we are free from the dominion or tyranny of present sins; we are free from the fear of future sin and slavery. We are free to enter the glorious adventure of faith and love in Christ's imperishable kingdom.

The followers of Christ have been called "the terrible meek," a tribute to the abiding strength of a meekness which their King brought to this earth. In the fellowship of His sufferings there lies even now a hidden glory which one day will overwhelm and consume all pomp and pretense of power and will usher us into the fullness of everlasting glory

The Hunter God

> *Blessed are those servants, whom the*
> *Lord when he cometh shall find watch-*
> *ing: verily I say unto you, that he shall*
> *gird himself, and make them sit down*
> *to meat, and shall come and serve them.*
> LUKE 12:35ff.

God is not an austere judge in the sky who loves
to throw the book at all evil doers. He is not a
capricious old uncle who loves to be pampered
with praise and sacrifice. He is not an exalted
landlord who has tenanted His world with crawl-
ing and cowering slaves. Nor is He a kindly and
venerable grandfather who absent-mindedly over-
looks the shame and reproach of His children.

God is a hunter Who pursues man relentlessly
with His justice and His love. He is a lover Who
woos and courts the favor of man. He is a rescuer
Who suffers and dies to save man from his sins.
He is a servant Who rolls up His sleeves and waits
tables at the heavenly banquet for us, His
children.

There is no other religion in all the world that

has had the incredible audacity and boldness to picture God as a seeker—a lover—a savior—a servant.

Christ is the King of heaven and earth. And what a strange and wondrous King! Can you imagine an earthly king, say Louis XIV of France, waiting tables in his castle at Versailles, except in royal jest? Normally the king is the *sought one,* someone people seek out for patronage or favors. He is the *adored one,* the high person to whom love and adoration are due and given. He is the *served one,* to whom hundreds and thousands give their service and protection.

The Bible sketches the Great King in a daring reversal of roles. "God so loved the world, that he gave his only begotten son . . . ." ". . . he humbled himself and took the form of a servant . . . ." ". . . he will make them sit down to meat, and will come and serve them."

Certainly the heart of man should leap in joy to meet such a King. And yet, think of the millions who hearing of Him, reject Him in unbelief or indifference. Should we not be overjoyed that He pursues us, and that we will be found of Him? Ought it not be wonderful to know that He waits to serve us? Should it not be of supreme comfort to realize that we are being loved of Him?

Perhaps you do not like to be hunted. The prospect of being pursued, or sought, may be comforting or discomforting, depending on the disposition of your heart. A few weeks ago two teen-age girls ran away from their South Dakota homes, and a week later sought out the police in a Texas city to surrender themselves. The first five days they were harassed by the thought that a hunt was on for them: they did not want to be found. But the seventh day they were fed up with wandering and actually desired to be found. Whittaker Chambers, the star witness at the Alger Hiss treason trial, described how for years he lived in fear of the hunt that might disclose his past, and how gradually he came to long for the hunt to be on so that his whole questionable past might be brought into the full light of inquiry and truth. It is so with man and his God. Until a man is awakened to the deep distress of his journey on the path of self-will, he will shun the hunter. Awakened, he will be stirred by strange longings and yearnings to be hunted, and to be found.

Francis Thompson in *The Hound of Heaven* expresses the poignant biography of a soul pursued:

I fled Him, down the nights and down the days:
I fled Him down the arches of the years;
. . . I hid from Him . . . up vistaed hopes I sped . . .
From those strong Feet that followed, followed after . . .
That Voice is round me like a bursting sea . . .
"Lo, all things fly thee, for thou fliest Me!"

Adam, fallen into sinful ways, fled Him. And man, by nature the child of wrath, runs away from God. Were God not a hunter, man would forever be lost. But man, by inclination, does not want a hunter God. Cardinal Newman confesses, "I loved to choose and see my path," and adds "but now, lead Thou me on!" It requires a profound change in the natural heart of man to surrender the wanderings of his own choosing and yield to the seeking, guiding hand of God.

Perhaps you do not like to be served. After all, you may cherish an independent self-reliance which scorns the need of being served. You dislike being a beggar; you can paddle your own canoe and pay your own way. None of us likes a fawning, conniving favor-seeker. And to be reduced to the role of the pauper with hands outstretched for help, even the help of God, is a disconcerting plight.

We are a people who boast a rugged individualism. To be told that dependence is our measure of spiritual maturity sounds a strange note. But man is great, not in terms of the proud independence of his life, but in terms of the humility of his acknowledged dependence. The Apostle said, "When I am weak, then am I strong." For a person to forget the basic dependence of his creatureliness, and to pretend to have the independence which ultimately belongs alone to God is to become at once a comic and a tragic figure.

It is as if a person pretends to fly by flapping his arms as wings; if he does it for his children's amusement, he is funny; but if he does it in utter seriousness, he is tragically demented, and needs to be hospitalized. If you get ambitions to fly, you had better recognize your dependence on an airplane, and seek the service of some airline.

However much it may pain our pride, we ought to recognize our need of being served. Existence itself, our very life, is ours because the Creator has served us with life. Every moment of every day we have the power of mind and the energy of body, the air we breathe and the food we eat, through the favor or sufferance of God. Moreover, our status in the Kingdom of God we have wholly through the grace which Christ's redemption gives us. By nature we are beggars all; our powers and rights we have as gifts from the Lord, our divine Servant.

Strangely enough, you may even resent being loved. The great news that "God so loved the world, that he gave his only begotten son . . ." may be more terrifying than comforting. Love is a conquering power. It breaks barriers and welds new loyalties. And you may not want that at all. If you have had a persistent lover, you may know such fears. You may have tried to discourage him, avoid him and resist him. If he continues still to woo you, you may actually become frightened—frightened over the prospect that you may capitulate to his love, and your whole life may be changed. Christ's love of you may be the most dreaded threat to your way of life imaginable. Should you surrender, you would be captive to the most transforming power on earth.

It could be that you would like a less meddlesome God, One who does not pursue, nor knock, nor woo—One rather who would barricade himself behind laws and requirements and leave you alone.

The altogether beautiful story of Christmas is the story of the God who did not leave you alone but who long ago came to visit the earth with His redemption. The altogether unique hope for the present is the message that this God continues to enter every trembling heart with His transforming work in repentance and faith. The altogether exhilarating prospect for the future is the promise that one day He will come again to complete His work in a blaze of consummate glory.

The present would be drab and hopeless indeed were it not that we live against the background of that first Christmas. His coming long ago is His guarantee that He comes today. Be sure that He who gave His life because He loved us so would not suffer a lapse of memory and forget the people He died to redeem. He is the eternal contemporary. A great company of transformed people form a parade through every generation, witnessing to the gracious visitation of Jesus Christ.

Henry Stanley, a great British journalist, was sent by his newspaper to Africa to discover David Livingstone and to record his exploits. Stanley went to find an explorer; he found an amazing person whom he could appraise only in this way: "Here is a man who is manifestly sustained as well as guided by influences from heaven. The Holy Spirit dwells in him. God speaks through him. The heroism, the nobility, the pure and stainless enthusiasm at the root of his life come beyond question from Christ. There must therefore be a Christ and it is worth while to have such a helper and a redeemer as this Christ undoubtedly is, as He reveals Himself in this wonderful disciple." A host of others, far less spectacular than Livingstone, devout mothers and unheralded fathers whose names never reach the press, make up this parade of transformed people who have been hunted and found, loved and redeemed, saved and served by our Lord.

What mood shall we have, what attitude or disposition, as we face this wondrous story? "Blessed are those servants whom the Lord when He cometh shall find watching," said Jesus. We are to watch—to be expectant—to entertain wonderfully unlimited hope. Life must march out from that first Christmas into a teeming, limitless present, and up toward the heights of an incredible future. If God is a hunter, anything can happen! How this distressed twentieth century needs this flight of hope. We who are all snarled up in the grim movements of history which threaten such sure disaster—we stand in pathetic need of some ray of hope. And this is more than a ray. It is the light of the world.

Let us pause in our furtive chase, for we are being hunted. Let us listen, because He is knocking. Let us yield our hearts to His loving. Let us take our places in boldness at His table, for He comes to serve us.

Taking Stock of Life

> *Thanks be unto God for his unspeak-*
> *able gift.*   II CORINTHIANS 9:15

The beginning of another year is a time for inventory. You take stock of yourself and of your world. Instead of attempting to help you with some long list of assets and liabilities, I point you to one item which you may quite overlook. It is more than another item among others in a series. In fact, to make any sort of inventory without including this gift may make your list hardly worth the bother.

I refer to that which Christmas gave to the world. Over nineteen centuries ago the world found itself with Jesus Christ on its hands. Since then, in taking stock of itself, the world has been unable to exclude Him from its calculations. Every man who has faced the claims that Jesus made for Himself and the claims which His followers have made for Him has had to come to terms with Him. He has been labelled "God." An "item" with such a label on your shelves makes the matter of inventory a rather baffling one. If the label is right, the price tag will be something fabulous. In fact, it probably ought to be priced higher than all the rest of the stock taken together. Any merchant will be ill at ease to have some one item on his shelves of more value than all the rest of the store. At least, he will remain disturbed until he takes adequate precaution to protect this one thing.

Life often takes on the aspect of a shop, and often a person suspects that some devilish prankster has broken in at night to interchange the price tags. That which is precious is thrown on a bargain counter and sold for a mess of pottage; that which is trash we clutch and grasp with life passion. Our inventories become a fool's audit. And, by all odds the gravest error in the world's continuous inventory is its casual and careless treatment of Christ. For, if the label is correct, in Him we have that item of such worth that the business of life depends on Him. With Him life is solvent; without Him, it is bankrupt.

Have you ever pondered what is implied in the good news that God so loved the earth that He gave His Only Begotten Son? In the first place, it implies that God's love of man was just about as great as any love can be. If any of you have an only son, you will know that to give your son would be harder than to give yourself. There can be no greater measure of love than is implied in this gift of the only begotten son. Jesus Christ, if we seriously take Him to be the Only Son of God, becomes our guarantee that God loves us.

But more is implied in this gift. It discloses something about man, too. If a friend of yours at Christmas received a portfolio of Beethoven's scores, you would have to conclude one of two things: either your friend must be a skilled musician, who has the capacity to use and enjoy the gift, or if he knows no music the person who gave him the gift has made a very stupid blunder. Jesus once told His disciples that they should not cast pearls to swine; hogs enjoy corn, not jewels. The fact that God gave His only Begotten Son to us puts the alternative squarely before us: either we are creatures with infinite capacities to receive and enjoy Christ and an unseen Kingdom, or Almighty God has made a most stupid blunder.

I know of nothing which has so shaken mankind to its roots as the Gospel, the glad tidings of God's gift of Christ, the Savior. It has not shaken him with terror, but with the staggering implications of the gift. What worth must man have if God gave him such a gift! You cannot escape the logic of such giving. Follow, if you will, the path of progress in human dignity and enterprise these centuries. Where have universities and hospitals sprung up? Where have the arts and sciences prospered? Where have governments shaken the shackles of tyranny and oppression, and made way for the rights of man? Always in the paths cleared first by the missionary! When man hears and believes the incredible information that the Everlasting God has held him in such high regard and worth that He gave to him His Only Begotten Son, there is only one course open to him. He cannot grovel as a slave any longer; if a Kingdom is his, he had better get on his feet and rule.

You and I, members of a civilization with centuries of Christian tradition, may take our dignity for granted. With scarcely a thought for how such convictions came to be, we accept our personal and civil rights as if they had always been self-evident. The fact is that they were never self-evident. Not until God disclosed them by showing us how much worth we had by giving us Jesus Christ—not until then did the men of history ever take seriously the rights of life, liberty and the pursuit of happiness. The rights of labor could never have become real except in the path of the Gospel, nor will they remain real apart from the continued connections with the Gospel. Democracy as a political ideal is sheer nonsense interpreted against any other philosophy of man than that which the Gospel gives; and, separated from the continuous leaven of the Gospel, Democracy is certain to be swallowed up by new tyrannies.

Whenever you set yourself to the task of making inventory of our assets as men, you will do violence to the facts if you do not place at the top of the list the matter of your Christian faith. Leave it out, or lump it with the miscellany of life, and you are on the way to going out of business. For this whole enterprise of the kind of life which Western Civilization at its best has flowered is founded upon the splendid implications of the Gospel of Jesus Christ.

A priceless gift has its awesome aspects too. It is disconcerting to have the gift on your hands if you do not have any inclination to want it. If you do not want to be children of God, it is a nuisance to have God knocking at your door with adoption papers in His hands. If you do not want a Kingdom and palaces, it can be terribly irksome to have someone hovering around trying to put a crown on your head. Of course, God will not force the issue. But, ever since Bethlehem this old world has stirred uneasily having the Gift of Christ and a beckoning Kingdom to deal with. We have gotten attached to the hovels, and the palace looks quite austere. We have settled down to being bell-hops to our passions and public opinion, and do not like to be disturbed by Christ's announcement that we were created for rulership.

Only two options are open to us. We may either receive the Gift for our use and enjoyment, or we

may exchange it for something else. We cannot
return it, for the Kingdom of the Christ is here
to stay. Thousands, like Esau of old, exchange the
rights of their high station for matters of the
moment. The stamp of intrinsic royalty which
Christ's coming has given you, you cannot renounce. Never again can you return to the common, menial rank of mere animal life. You are
now of the nobility, but you may be a nobleman
in rebellion. The powers of mind and heart which
you have are at once sublime and terrible, sublime
if arrayed on the side of God, terrible if pitted
against Him. To exchange the divine potential of
your Christ-redeemed self for that which is trivial
and base is more than folly or stupidity; it is high
treason in heavenly places. A peasant may rebel
without disturbing the state; but when the son
of the king rebels, it shakes the kingdom. You and
I are no longer peasants in the universe; by
creation and redemption we are heirs of the Kingdom. It is therefore that the injustice and avarice
of men can destroy the earth and wring the heart
of heaven. If man exchanges this Christ for gods
of his own making, if he chooses rulership over
machines and men instead of rulership over his
own will and mind, if he employs his divine
capacities for power instead of prudence, for
money instead of morals, for gain instead of goodness, then he will bring down upon himself the
disaster and the shame of eternity.

The other option is as sublime as this one is base. God will give us the power to receive His priceless gift in Christ, the gift of forgiveness and holiness, and will enable us to enjoy His Kingdom, here and forever. To this end were we created, and for this purpose the gift of grace was given. Surmounting all the dazzling inventories of time is God Himself. Were we to gain the whole world, and miss God, we would be paupers still. Possessing God, though all else were to go, the Kingdom would still be ours.

You Cannot Escape God

> *Whither shall I go from thy spirit? or whither shall I flee from thy presence? If I ascend up into heaven, thou art there: if I make my bed in hell, behold, thou art there. If I take the wings of the morning, and dwell in the uttermost parts of the sea; Even there shall thy hand lead me, and thy right hand shall hold me.* PSALM 139

There are many things in life you hope to escape. And, if you are lucky, you may succeed. Most of us have escaped famine; few of us have gone to bed hungry because we have had to. Most of us, perhaps all, have escaped blindness, insanity or other major disabilities of life. And many a person has escaped ill health his whole life through, and has had the end come with such swiftness that it could almost be said that he had escaped any conscious encounter with death itself.

One you cannot escape: *God!* You may reject Him, defy Him, ignore Him and neglect Him,

23

but you cannot escape Him. You may surrender to His gentle, strong arms of mercy, or you may wriggle and squirm in His mighty grip of judgment, but you cannot escape Him.

The saddest and strangest quality of the human being is his deep inclination to run away from God. We who were made for the ultimate purpose of living with Him, we turn from Him. Like branches detached from the tree, we wither and die without Him, yet we cut ourselves off from Him. Dying of hunger, we refuse food; routed and defeated in battle, we refuse reinforcements and victory; troubled and distraught, we refuse peace; condemned and dying, we refuse pardon and life. Is there any more tragic spectacle than this: man refusing God?

The obvious reason for this flight from God is the suspicion that He is an angry God. Nor is this hunch wrong. He is an angry God. But, would you want Him otherwise? What sort of being would you have on your hands if He had no capacity for indignation or wrath? As men we fail to be like God in two respects: we have neither His love nor His anger. There is a time for mercy, and there is a time for wrath. The capacity for the one implies a capacity for the other. A mother whose son is enslaved to drink and lust most likely will hate the smell of alcohol and sensuousness in art with all her being, simply because she loves her son. We often hear people say, "If there is a God, why does He allow wars?"—which is really equivalent to saying, "Why does not God let the world get by with its greed, selfishness, indifference and lust?" The fact is that if He is God, He cannot let unrighteousness go unpunished. And wars are a corporate punishment for corporate wrongs. Would we want a God who is a sleepy, old dullard, and who with a couple of beers under his belt chuckles and thinks it cute when Cain kills Abel; and, when Cain later gets lonesome for Abel, buys him a Cadillac roadster to make him happy again? The fact is that if we want a God at all, we want an angry God.

We run away from God not because He is angry, but because we are sinful. The secret of our behavior lies not in that nature of God, but in the nature of man.

If you have not been running away from God in sheer terror of His judgment, you had better start running. You will need to face up to the double fact of God's anger and your own sinfulness.

Sin is rebellion. And the rebel flees. Before the fall, God walked with Adam in the cool of the evening. When Adam disobeyed God, he began at once to flee Him. And God, calling, "Adam, Adam, where art thou?" overtook him with the fearsome judgment of expulsion. For Jonah,

God's path lay toward Nineveh, but Jonah fled the Lord toward Tarshish; and God's wrath caught up with him in the belly of a fish. David abandoned God and chose his illicit tryst with Bathsheba; Jehovah's anger blazed at him through the accusing finger of Nathan the prophet. "Day and night thy hand was heavy upon me," confesses David, in describing his flight from the divine hand of judgment. Peter denied Him, and the infinite sadness of Jesus' eyes broke him. Judas betrayed Him, and the Lord's hand hurled him about to face his accomplices in the anguish of remorse. Paul fled Him until on the Damascus road Christ's words, "Saul, Saul, why persecutest thou me?" sent him reeling on to a life-long apostleship.

Millions of people could echo the words of the Psalmist, "Whither shall I flee from thy presence . . . if I take the wings of the morning and dwell in the uttermost parts of the sea, even there shall thy hand lead me, and thy right hand shall hold me." You cannot escape God.

One might ask whether the Psalmist is describing the dreadfulness of not being able to run away from God's anger, or whether he is affirming the reassuring wonder of not being able to drift out beyond the tender and strong reach of His love. Perhaps he is expressing a mixture of both motifs. It seems as if on the one hand, he seeks to hide from God.

> If I say, surely the darkness shall cover me;
> Even the night shall be light about me.
> Yea, the darkness hideth not from thee;
> But the night shineth as the day:
> The darkness and the light are both alike to thee.

And on the other hand, he voices the sublime comfort of God's ever-presence.

> In thy book all my members were written . . .
> How precious are thy thoughts unto me, O God!

A little boy does wrong, and tremblingly awaits the punishment of his father. If he is a little-enough boy, he may try to hide in the closet or under the bed. When he appears before his father, his eyes are filled with both fear and pathetic love. He is torn between running away and flinging his arms about his father. And after the spanking, his only comfort is to cling tightly to his father as he sobs himself into peace. For intuitively he knows that the hand that spanked him is the hand of his strongest love.

Is it not strange that fear and love can be so mingled? What is this great mystery, that we can be so repelled by God and so drawn to Him in the same moment?

The long history of men is one of running away from Him. The deep sinfulness of our hearts does not want Him around meddling. This Witness with the all-seeing eye—let us be rid of Him. You want to execute an unfair contract in busi-

ness, and hovering around is God! You want to
yield to illicit love, but three is a crowd, and you
cannot squeeze Him out. You feel sorry for yourself, and would like to simmer in your own burning self-pity, but there He stands, He who knows
all the false premises of your silly grief; and you
have no alternative but to become furiously
angry or to relax your passion in a sense of humor
over the ridiculous spectacle of your self-sorrow.
You succeed in getting the praise and homage of
the crowd, and would love to strut in happy self-
pride, but there stands One who knows all, and
quietly reminds you, "When you have done all,
say, I am an unprofitable servant." You simply
cannot bask in your ill-gotten gains, your stolen
loves, your sweet self-pity, or your swollen pride—
with Him around.

Now, what does He want with you? Why does
He torture you so? Cannot He leave you alone?

If you want an answer, look at Him. Look long.
You think He carries a whip. But it is not a whip
that makes His shoulders stoop so. Look again! It
is a cross that weighs down His frame. And those
hands that will not let you go, they have nail
prints in them. The eyes that fix you night and
day—they do not blaze in anger; they are filled
with tears.

The depth—the sadness—of God's anger lies in
His holy love. A man is faithless to his wife. One
woman may be spared anguish because he is not

her husband and she does not love him. His wife, though she loves him, may be spared anguish if she does not know of his faithlessness. Or, she may be spared, if like him, she too leads an illicit life. But God cannot be spared. For He loves, and He knows, and He is holy. How much easier if He could dismiss us and let us go.

Towering over the wrecks of time is a cross— the cross which tells the story of God's infinite anger and love—an anger that cannot forget and a love that cannot forsake. In that altogether strange and wondrous event in history, God's wrath hurled itself against all sin because it was the only way in which His love could redeem a fallen world. In Christ, the dying Savior, God was at work reconciling us to Himself. His wrath could not be tempered; the full punishment for sin must needs be administered and paid. In love, He took it upon Himself for us. He was "the Lamb of God that taketh away the sin of the world."

It is only beneath this cross that man stops running away from God. Standing there, we stop trying to be rid of Him. There we learn to love His will, the very law that would condemn. There we learn to walk in His paths, and rest in His abiding presence. Hearing His promise, "Lo, I am with thee alway," we learn to echo in ecstasy the Psalmist's reassuring lines, "Whither shall I flee from thy presence . . ."

What Is Faith?

*Now faith is the substance of things
hoped for, the evidence of things not
seen . . .*
*Through faith we understand that the
worlds were framed by the word of
God . . .*
*By faith Abel offered unto God a more
excellent sacrifice than Cain . . .*
*By faith Enoch was translated that he
should not see death . . .*
*By faith Abraham, when he was called
to go out . . . obeyed; and he went out,
not knowing whither he went.*

HEBREWS 11

The first thing to be said of faith is that you
cannot create it, achieve it nor win it. It is a gift
of God. Having said that, we hasten to add that
you will be held responsible for not having faith,
despite the fact that it is a gift. You cannot fly like
a bird either, but if you do not fly to New York
in the next ten hours it will be because you refuse
or neglect to take passage in something that can
and will fly you to New York. If you do not have
faith, it is simply because you decline or ignore
the gift of faith which is freely offered you. It is

offered without caprice or whim to one as unconditionally and impartially as to another.

The second thing to be said is that the offer of faith is pressed upon you each time you hear or read the Word of God. While we confess in Luther's classic words, "I believe that I cannot by my own reason or strength believe in Jesus Christ, my Lord, or come to Him," we also go on to affirm that ". . . the Holy Ghost has called me through the Gospel . . . ." At this very instant, as you hear the preaching of the Word, the Holy Ghost is at the door of your heart knocking, in the hope that He may come in with the glorious gift of faith. If you cease to resist, you will sense the quiet tread of His footfalls in your heart, and you will leave here with new peace and strength.

The third thing to be said is that the gift is given to the unresisting heart of a three weeks old child in Holy Baptism. We are inclined to conclude that the Lord's work in us depends on our conscious awareness, when the fact is that even in our adult years He conveys countless blessings of which we may be quite unaware. Who are you to limit the scope of God's activity? May it not be that this morning, even though you feel no spiritual ecstasy nor remember the content of the sermon—may it not be that you leave this hour of worship strangely and wondrously enriched by the Holy Ghost's work in your hearts? Let us suppose that a child of three

weeks is assigned a trust fund of a million dollars by a wealthy uncle in Australia. The fact
that the child is unaware of his sudden wealth
has no legal bearing on the fact that he is the
possessor of this money. The gift is his alone by
action of his uncle. It is so with faith. Whether
given to an infant in the Sacrament or to an unresisting Saul in the flaming consciousness of a
Damascus road, it is the initiative of a bestowing
Lord that assures us the gift.

The writer to the Hebrews opens this epic
recital of faith with these words, "Now faith is
the substance of things hoped for, the evidence
of things not seen." Christian faith has the mirac-
ulous power to change the vague, nebulous world
of hope to a pathway of firm rock. It transforms
the intangible kingdom of the unseen into a solid
certainty. Faith suffuses the entire person, mind,
heart and will, and enfolds all life with purpose
that defies death and blossoms in eternity.

By faith the mind is enabled to put God in
the center; it can understand that the world—
everything—was created by His almighty Word.
Faith gives the mind a key by which it can order
and arrange all the varied phenomena of existence. The mind is wise not alone in terms of
what it knows, but in terms of knowing what it
does not and cannot know. Socrates declared that
he had spent most of his life arriving at the
point where he knew that he did not know, and

that he hoped to spend the rest of his life staying there, so that he would not slip back into thinking that he knew. We easily confuse opinions, notions and hunches with fact or knowledge. A man is wise who knows that he does not know. Faith is God's gift to the mind, enabling it to take divine truths that cannot be discovered in laboratories or syllogisms and to live by them with a conviction that is more unchanging than a mathematical axiom. It is often a very convulsive experience indeed for the mind to surrender its proud pretense to know all things, and to yield to the gentle tutoring of faith. The man of faith will still find his world filled with the wondrous mystery of the unknown and unknowable, but his faith will give him assurance and conviction in the towering questions of life's purpose and meaning.

Faith works in man's heart to give him a new quality of love. It was not the difference of their gifts that made Abel's sacrifice of firstlings of the flock pleasing to God and Cain's sacrifice of grain displeasing. Abel brought the gift of a loving heart! Ordinarily we think of the heart of man as symbolic of something deeper and more decisive than his mind. A man may change his mind and be the same man; if he has had a change of heart we regard him as a changed man. The heart is the term used to describe the seat of a man's affections and loyalties. Now faith is that power from God which transforms and reshapes man's deeper emotions. It enables him to love both God and man.

Without a heart of love, man cannot please God, whatever outward tokens or works he may give. That which made Christ so severe in His invectives against the Pharisees was precisely this: they were meticulous in their outward religious disciplines without having the quality of love in their hearts. They substituted tokens for the real thing. Do you think a girl in love would be pleased to receive a dozen roses from the man she loved, if she knew that he did not love her and that he gave her flowers only out of pity? The roses, without his love, could only increase her anguish. Do you remember the words of the Master in Lowell's *The Vision of Sir Launfal?* In the opening scene the knight had in disdain thrown a coin to the begging leper; in the closing scene, years later, he had shared his remaining crust of bread with the leper. And the "Master" points out the difference:

> He who gives himself with his gift feeds three,
> Himself, his hungering neighbor and me.

But to give yourself to another with a loving heart, whether God or man, is a quality which God alone can give you, through the gift of faith.

By faith Abraham obeyed and went out, not knowing where he went. Faith issues in a new obedience of man's will. It not only makes him think different and feel different; it makes him live a different life. It makes him *do* something. You may believe that the world is round, or flat, and do nothing about it. A man may confess faith in communism and still live blissfully in the wealth of his capitalistic holdings. But if you have the quality of Christian faith which the Lord gives, the course of your whole life may change. You come under a new law, the law of love, and all the decisions of your life must shape themselves around this law as a center. You cannot go on as you were.

This new obedience begins with Jesus Christ. He gave His life on the cross for you. In Him you have the forgiveness of your sins and the promise of a life everlasting. Through faith, He takes up residence in your soul. And living within you, He pervades your whole being with a new spirit and a new law. You can go your heedless and selfish way no longer. Out of a new and radical gratitude to Him for your salvation, you turn to a glad search of His will and wishes. What He wills, you now will. What He asks, you do, whatever the risks may be. If He asks that you leave the safe and tried paths of your own family and land to become a missionary in a strange corner of the earth, you have no other option but to go. Or, if instead He asks that you relinquish some of your savings or earnings to make possible the work of His Kingdom, you have no choice but to surrender some of your financial security to take that risk for Him. If He bids you place the calling to promote and advance His Kingdom above the job by which you make a living, you have no alternative but to give time and thought and money to that which He regards of first importance. To do other is to disobey and renounce the very faith by which you are saved.

It is a perilous thing indeed to get involved in a gift which threatens to change so much of your life. If you want to go on untroubled in your easy and self-determined way, you had better turn away from both gift and Giver. But if you want your life to be caught up in something so wonderful that even death is scarcely an incident, as with Enoch, and something which will sustain you through all of life and usher you at last into an incredible eternity—then, let the Lord give you this faith!

The Temptation

> *And when the tempter came to him, he
> said, If thou be the Son of God, com-
> mand that these stones be made bread...
> Then the devil taketh him up into
> the holy city, and setteth him on a pin-
> nacle of the temple, And saith unto him,
> If thou be the Son of God, cast thyself
> down ...
> Again, the devil taketh him up into an
> exceeding high mountain, and sheweth
> him all the kingdoms of the world, and
> the glory of them; And saith unto him,
> All these things will I give thee, if thou
> wilt fall down and worship me.*
> MATTHEW 4:1-11

The most powerful symbol in the world is the
cross. In today's dramatic story, Satan proposes
to Jesus that He choose something other than
the symbol of suffering and shame. Why not
give mankind the symbol of the breadbasket or
granary—make stones into bread—be the world's
breadwinner! Or, give men some sensational
sign, like a magician's wand—throw yourself down
from the pinnacle of the temple and let the
angels pick you up! Or, if you would rather,

give them the symbol of the sword, something
man can easily understand—become the great
totalitarian ruler of men! Why choose a cross?
And let us remember, we who live in the twentieth century, to choose a cross in the first century would be as if someone today were to choose
a hangman's noose. The years have surrounded
the cross with a sublime history of mercy, adventure and sacrifice, so that its offense is today
largely gone. But in first century Palestine the
cross was the cruelest and most shameful device
for doing away with criminals.

What if He had heeded the tempter and de-
serted the cross? Can you imagine hundreds of
millions today singing in ecstasy,

> Onward, Christian soldiers, marching as to war,
> With the sword of Jesus going on before?

Or, would a great church be built on the refrain,

> In the granaries of Christ I glory,
> Towering o'er the wrecks of time?

Or, would anyone be singing today,

> All hail the power of Jesus' Name,
> Let angels prostrate fall,

if the most notable thing He did was to throw
Himself down from the temple in sensational act,
or make wine from water, or even raise Lazarus

from the dead? What chance would He have had with any other symbol but the cross?

He elected to make His bid for the world through a cross. If that failed, then He would fail. He would not be a great provider, nor a dazzling magician, nor a mighty dictator. He rejected all alternatives. For Him it would be a cross! to p. 42

Let us not dismiss the alternatives quickly. The pattern of the Lord's temptation is a repeating one. If some leader, or a program of action, or a course of life has as its credentials, its appeal, economic plenty or sensational mystery or spectacular power, we human beings are prone to be immensely impressed.

Under a myriad of forms the temptation to exchange one's soul for bread continues to capture men. A man may surrender his freedom for security, compromise his honor for gain. Political parties stay in power if they can maintain a high economic level of life, and lose the election if their program calls for economic sacrifice. The bid which communism is making for the world is basically the promise of bread. Many a man shrugs off his unworthy deeds by protesting, "A man has got to live, doesn't he?" The Lord's maxim, "Man shall not live by bread alone" is regarded valid only for the man who has riches enough to assure him bread. Carlyle said that not all the "Finance Ministers and Upholsterers and Confectioners of modern Europe . . . in joint stock company" could "make one shoeblack happy . . . above an hour or two." But whatever the essayists may say about happiness, the masses will follow the man who can promise bread.

   We need not disguise the fact that this temptation has a fierce appeal for all of us. Nor was the Lord Himself unmindful of our need of bread. He who preached about the bread of life also fed the multitudes bread and fish, and warned His followers that when a man came asking bread you could not discharge your divine obligation to him with a dish of pious prattle. However, He made it clear that if man had all the bread needed, he would still have hungers which if left unsatisfied would leave his life famished and barren.

   If the promise of security has its appeal, so also has the promise of the sensational. We are easily beguiled by novelty. Life is full of wonder, it is true, and if we have eyes to see we shall find incredible mystery and magic in the commonplace, like the design of a snowflake and the color of a sunset. But we are peculiarly drawn to tricksters and charlatans.

   In the religious realm the temptation to follow wonder-workers is peculiarly strong. For, the power of God is limitless and the quality of the unpredictable is native to religious life. We forget that faith is at its best when it is not buttressed by divine stunts, for faith is ". . . the conviction of things not seen." And if the only way we can keep going is to have God fling a miracle in our path at every turn, our life is not of faith at all. True, Christ did perform miracles, but out of kindness and mercy, and not for the purpose of bracing up a paralytic faith. Faith comes by the Word of God, and not through some celestial three-ring-circus.

Do you think our congregation would serve God and our people better if we were able to announce that each Sunday morning some new miracle would be performed in the chancel? What real good could be achieved if I could this morning cause a new automobile to appear out of nothing, or if next Sunday I could bring back from the local hospital a cancer patient and restore him to health? With an announced schedule of weekly miracles we could doubtless have people cramming every corner of the church and clamoring for reservations for next Sunday's "show." But, I ask you, what abiding good would we be doing for people?

Nor let anyone say we are not impressed by power. We pin our hopes for the survival of our nation and civilization on the ability to amass greater power than our rivals. We measure our personal successes in terms of our competitive ability to outrank our fellows. He who longs and yearns for truth we dismiss as a dreamer; he who can get things done and who can "put it over" elicits our praise. This universal desire to be pre-eminent is mankind's recurring temptation. Jesus abandoned a throne to choose a cross; we alto-gether too often sidestep a cross to gain some little throne.

With terrifying clarity, Feodor Dostoevsky in *The Brothers Karamazov* describes the issues of the Lord's temptation, and indicts the medieval church with the charge of having capitulated to the lures of "the wise one." Under the guise of correcting the work of Jesus, the *Grand Inquis-itor* proposes that the church has set out to cap-ture man by bread, magic and political power. And there are shameful chapters in the history of the church when this literally has been done. In certain periods of its history, there are nations that have had three-fourths of their lands owned by the church and have had to rely on the church for bread. There are other epochs when the church by means of relics, shrines and miracle-cures have held people in bondage to the mys-terious. And there have been periods when the church has been politically so strong that it has appointed and deposed kings. But these have not been the periods of the church's glory.

The church, like her Master, must win and rule from the cross. To rely on any lesser symbol betrays her Lord. And we who bear the Lord's name, Christians, bear purest witness when in our daily lives we detach ourselves from the pull of these repeating temptations and take up our cross and follow Him.

This temptation of Jesus takes on added significance when we recall that it was a part of the devil's deliberate strategy to prevent Jesus from going to His death. Satan did not want Jesus to die. If by wooing Him away from this redemptive death or if by terrifying Him with the prospects of suffering, Satan could deflect Him from His atoning mission, the world would still be held captive by the enemy. Had Jesus capitulated to the persuasions of Satan, not only would this great and good Jesus have fallen; the salvation of the world would have failed. We would yet be in our sins.

Jesus was tempted in all points as we are tempted. In a fuller sense than for any of us, He was *man*. Death was not less terrifying for Him than for you; in fact, because He was a man in all the fullness of manhood, death for Him was more fraught with dread than for you. But, tempted and terrified as He was, He went unflinching to His death, for you and for me.

It remains for us to thank Him ceaselessly; and in the redemption which He provided it is for you and me to follow Him here, and through death into everlasting life

The History of a Man

For the bread of God is that which cometh down out of heaven, and giveth life unto the world. They said therefore unto him, Lord, evermore give us this bread. Jesus said unto them, I am the bread of life: he that cometh to me shall never hunger, and he that believeth on me shall never thirst. JOHN 6:33-35

There are two ways to write the history of a man. One is to measure his years against the world of nature into which he was born and in which he lived and died—

He was born of strong stock.

He grew up with good food and shelter and schools.

He married well and had four children.

He was successful in wresting from the world a good living and amassed a modest fortune of $75,000.00.

He battled pneumonia, diabetes and a kidney infection.

At seventy-seven, he succumbed to old age and was buried.

There you have his history from womb to tomb. His story is told in terms of his striving with the elements of his environment, with nature and with his world

The other way to write his history is to begin at a point beyond his birth, and say that while he had two parents and entered the world through the normal process of birth, he actually was created by God and was dispatched into this world by Him. You go on to write the history of his years, not in terms of his interaction with the elements of his environment, but in terms of his dealings with God. The most significant facts in his years are not his diet, his bodily metabolism, his professional progress, the number of his children, the skill with which he grappled old mother nature for a living, nor the length of his years. As he moved across the stage of time, the real drama of his life was his encounter and transactions with One other towering Figure on the stage—God. His story is the story of two characters, God and man, as they moved through one scene and act after another.

Observe this man. When he took the stage as a romantic lover did he ad lib in the hubbub of the crowd, or did he play the lines over against the other silent Figure, the Lover of his soul?

When he hit the act called "prosperity," was he carried off by the glitter of the stage trappings, or did he walk and speak humbly as a steward?

When the play led on into the valley of great decision, did he conform his lines to the noble will of that wise and benevolent Partner on the stage?

When he had to face that difficult scene of loss and loneliness, did he give way to melancholy and despair, or did he make the scene a memorable one by taking his cue from the great Friend who had great lines of courage and hope ready for the hour?

When the fury of temptation broke in upon him and the whole stage trembled with the gigantic forces pitted for his soul, did he go down to defeat in fear and shame, or did he team up with this mighty Lord of Hosts and make the scene an unforgettable episode of victory, driving the tempters off the stage in riot?

And when the curtain came slowly down on the last act, did he slink off like a "quarry slave at night scourged to his dungeon," or, arm in arm with the great Partner of the play, did he move into the wings with eyes aglow, with the promise of the eternal Oscar, the crown, awaiting him?

There is more to life than meets the eye. The bread of life is not only wheat. Man is more than body, and his world more than black earth and blue water. The forces that play in the drama of his years are not only economic and political, biological and chemical. His destiny is not only to be born on one end and die on the other.

There is a great unseen plot waiting to unfold in the story of every man. And in that plot there are the two great figures, God and you. If you miss Him, then you are in Shakespeare's words, "a poor player who struts and frets his hour upon the stage, and then is heard no more." But if you play it out with God, then whatever the earthly critics may say in their vague reviews, the story of your life will take its place in the glorious libraries of heaven.

This stirring prospect would only be bitter disillusion were it not true that God is on the stage. If He were a spectator, cheering you on or jeering you down, He would only make your performance more difficult. If He were a critic, coldly regarding you from some box seat far off in the heavens, you would have no heart. Even if He were in the wings, prompting you in the rough spots it would not be enough.

But the glad, good news of the Gospel is that He is right in the thick of the play, every minute on the stage. For thirty-three years He let Himself be seen by human eyes. Peter and the others heard His voice, felt the touch of His hand, saw the tears in His eyes. Then one day, He wrapped around Him the cloak of invisibility, and announced that henceforth He would be as fully and powerfully there as before, but now we should have to see and hear and touch Him with the faculty of faith. And on the stage of time He left the strange imprint of a Cross in which every player of faith would find renewal through forgiveness of sins and grace for every hour.

In recent years it has been the habit of many historians to describe this human drama in terms of economics, the struggle for this world's goods. Man's elemental need is bread, or food. The rise and fall of civilizations are measured by the accessibility of bread. And indeed, much can be said for this formula as the key to life. A people whose soil is allowed to erode and whose natural resources are squandered eventually will rob their children's children not only of bread, but of the arts and sciences too. Not only the world's armies but their civilizations too, advance on their stomachs.

Of all religions, Christianity has been most concerned about bread, and has been berated as a materialistic faith. Jesus did anguish over men's bodily wants and pains. But He warned His people that in the long stretch men's bodily wants would not be met if they did not first seek the Kingdom of God and His righteousness. It was after He had fed the five thousand with five barley loaves and two fish that He spoke to them of the bread of God and called Himself the bread of life. If men wrestled only with mother nature to win the abundance of things, man himself would become debased, and his whole life go wrong. If like other animals he struggles primarily for food, his life even as an animal will go brutal and be destroyed. Man was placed on this earth not primarily to win over his physical environment, to conquer the soil and the seas, but to come to grips with the eternal God and win an eternal Kingdom. For that reason, man does not live by bread alone, but by the Word that comes from God.

The heartening thing at this point is that if we have a profound need for this heavenly bread, this sustenance from an eternal kingdom, the supply is bountifully at hand. The celestial Bread became flesh and dwelt among us. Jesus, the living Word, took the form of a servant; He became our brother in the flesh. He entered the warp and woof of the sinful, fallen order, and as the Sinless One went to His death to become our Redeemer and Savior. Here we face the mystery of mysteries. As with the phenomenon of electricity, we stand baffled and bewildered to define its strange essence, but we go on to use its power nonetheless.

How a death on Golgotha's cross could free a world from sin we are helpless to know. But faith takes hold of the incredible corollaries of this event and lives by them. God and man are reconciled, and you have a right to play out this drama of life with the Mighty God. He no longer hovers inaccessible in the wings but, incarnate, is in the thick of the play. You need not look furtively for help, because He is at your very elbow. If you sin, He forgives; if you fall, He lifts; if you seek, He finds you.

In the hour of doubt, He reassures you with His promises: I have sent thee—I have given thee a name—I have redeemed thee—thou art Mine. He has really cast you in this significant role, and won your right to it. Your life, long or short, has eternal significance. If a lamb is born into a flock, frolics gaily for a fortnight in the meadows, then dies before it can be sheared for wool or cut into chops, the lamb is said to have missed its purpose, its destiny. It is not so with you. Had you died with your first breath, the drama is still full and complete: you came from God, and you return to God.

In the hour of great sorrow, when the heart is heavy with loneliness or broken by a betrayed love, then He comes with His tender and gentle touch to soothe the convulsed spirit and cool the fevered brow.

In the hour of shame and sin, when guilt descends like a darkening cloud and blocks out the sun, then the glorious light of His Cross, His wondrous forgiveness, breaks through the gloom and ushers in the eternal peace.

In the hour of success and plenty, when you feel the power of competence and the thrill of achievement, and your head grows a bit giddy over your own importance, He comes to guard you against pride and complacency, those deadly enemies which in unguarded moments can destroy your soul.

Every man's life will carry him across the stage of time through many acts and scenes—through comedy and tragedy, through want and plenty, through sickness and health, through friendship and loneliness.

If the plot of your life winds in and out of the Person and Will of your Lord and Savior, you will play out the great drama of life abundant, and as you enter the wings you will be ushered upon a new and eternal stage with an incredible plot and role waiting you.

Return to What?

> *Let the wicked forsake his way, and the*
> *unrighteous man his thoughts: and let*
> *him return unto the Lord, and he will*
> *have mercy upon him; and to our God,*
> *for he will abundantly pardon.*
>
> ISAIAH 55:7

It is noteworthy that the Bible often uses the word *return*. To return, or to go back, is not altogether a popular cry, least of all in this twentieth century with its worship of progress. We have learned to exalt that which is new or modern, until we often assume that because a thing is new it therefore must be better than that which is old. A new book, a new fashion, a new friend, a new wife must necessarily be an advance over the former. So we press on in adventure and anticipation for something novel.

There are people who disclaim this god, progress, and just as foolishly extol that which is old. They speak of "the good old days," as if the old days were all good. They praise the simple life of the pioneers, as if life was so much simpler when drinking-water had to be carried in a pail. They see greatness in people who are dead and gone, but regard their neighbor as stupid and immoral. They fill their rooms with warped antiques and their minds with wistful memories.

Then there are people who make a worship of status quo. The present order of things is the best. They disdain the past, they fear future changes as revolutionary. They want neither the hard road back nor the perilous road forward. They have neither the repentance required for turning around and going backward, nor have they the gallantry required for pressing on and going forward. So they sit smugly by, protesting any change.

Whatever your temperament may be, the fact is that the prophets of the Lord were unanimous in calling on the people to return. Not to some golden age in the past, however. The call was always to return to the Lord. And that is a long cry from a return to some vague, idealized past. It is the journey of the soul back to the Creator who made him and the Savior who redeemed him. It is not a retreat back to some antiquity in time and place; it is a turning about from a Godlessness which, whether ancient or modern, is a wasteland of the spirit. And, since the journey leads to God, it ushers the soul into adventures and enterprises that never grow old.

To return, in that type of journey, is a more rigorous and exacting passage than any other. For it implies that a man has been going in the wrong direction and that he faces squarely the folly and sinfulness of his ways. Isaiah gives this preface, "Let the wicked forsake his way and the unrighteous man his thoughts." Then let him return to the Lord. How much more palatable to our pride if he had said, "Press on to God, you gallant ones." But he said, return! Take the road of sorrow and penitence, abandon the position of self-sufficiency which you have held so smugly, creep on your hands and knees back to the God whom you have dishonored and forgotten so long. There is no other road to God, but the road back. Recall Christ's striking parable of the Pharisee and the Publican. The Pharisee tried pressing on up the slopes of his own meritorious deeds; the Publican took the via dolorosa of repentance. The Pharisee succeeded only in losing his way further in the thickets of conceit; the Publican found God.

One of the great figures of the ancient world was Constantine, emperor of Rome in the fourth century. Most of us remember how he had a vision of the cross in the sky, and considering it an auspicious sign, embroidered the cross on all his banners, and swept down the Alps with his armies to overwhelm Maxentius and conquer Rome. Every history book relates how he became the first royal patron and protector of Christendom. Persecutions ceased, and the cross of Christ entered the court of the Caesars. But the real encounter between Constantine and Christ came much later, when after thirty years as a defender of Christendom, he made that personal pilgrimage of the soul, and knelt one day in the nave of the church of St. Lucian the Martyr to confess his sins and be baptized. Before the bishops of the east, he laid aside the purple toga of the empire to be robed in the white of a disciple of the Christ. He never again donned the royal robe, and later, surrounded by his generals at his bedside, he said, "I have only one wish now. I have won pardon and peace. I only seek to hasten my journey to God." He had offered much to the Christian Church those thirty years, but he learned at last that the one thing needful was to offer simply the sacrifice of the broken heart, the contrite spirit. Constantine the Great had made his return to God. The mighty and the weak alike must take this road if they are to find God.

The return to God, moreover, means the recovery of elemental truths that on any other path are easily lost. The whole world today is in danger of pinning its hopes on group action. Vast millions look to the rising power of the workers for prosperity and peace. Others, in fear of these new economic blocs, cry for the survival of political democracy. Still others, especially in

the United States and Great Britain, hope for
the resurgence of the capitalistic forms of the last
two centuries. Whatever form it may take, the
world at large is reaching out frantically for some
organization, some balance among classes and nations which may keep tensions and conflict of
rival interests from collapsing into chaos and
bloodshed.

In our eager search, we largely forget the truth,
which ought to be quite obvious, that real power
is spiritual rather than physical. The power of
evil, or sin, is of the spirit; the power of good,
the hope of the world, is of the spirit too. Shifting power from one group or class to another is
but a masquerade, if the quality of that power is
not changed from evil to good. Greed in the
hands of the workers is as destructive as greed
in the hands of the owners. The Bible records
an instance where a slave, Onesimus, had gone
on a strike against his owner, Philemon. The
apostle Paul pleads with Philemon to forgive
and restore Onesimus. Slavery was an economic
and social institution with grave faults. But Paul
apparently regards the chief problem not one
of the shifting of power from Philemon to Onesimus, but that whoever had the power use it
charitably and mercifully. He wanted Philemon,
who had the power under that system, to remember that his slave, who had no power, was still
a human being who, under God their common

Creator, should be regarded, with himself, as a child of God. Were Paul to live today, he might plead with workers, in their world-wide rise to power, to remember that the owners were human beings, and should be treated as children of God. Up and down the streets of every city and village today the arguments go on, pro and con. Labor has too much power, say some. Capital has too much power, say others. Government has too much power, say still others. To each man the chief problem appears to be the juggling of this power, from one group to another, depending on the particular prejudice he may have. All the while, the truth of God is that simply to shift power neither destroys it nor changes it. The only hope is that some of this power, whoever chances to have it, may undergo a qualitative change from evil to good. Power is spiritual, in the profoundest sense, and only a spiritual shifting of it will effect any lasting change in the life of man on the earth. We need desperately to return to God for this truth, if we are to help this old world.

We need to recapture the truth that wealth, too, is of the spirit. What you have in your heart is eternal; what you have in your hands is temporal. Lloyd Douglas in his book, *White Banners,* tells of a man who in 1929 had his money swept away overnight. Tossing sleeplessly in a hospital bed on the brink of nervous collapse, he repeated over and over, "They have taken my money." A dear friend who knew where real wealth lay, said to him, "Thomas, they have taken your money, but don't let them take your sleep too." Then she led him to see that if he let God remove the rancour and hatred from his heart, they could not rob him of peace, the treasure of the heart. Booker T. Washington, the great Negro who founded Tuskegee Institute, once said, "No man, either white or black, from North or South, shall drag me down so low as to make me hate him." The fortunes of circumstance may fill your hands, or empty them; but they can neither enrich nor rob your heart. To be impoverished there is of your own doing; to be rich there is a matter between you and God. And if you have let the Lord fill that heart of yours, no power on earth or under the earth can break in to plunder and rob. Moth or rust cannot corrupt, nor thieves break in and steal.

On Mars' hill Paul faced the speculative philosophers of ancient Athens with the tantalizing suggestion: The Lord is not far from any one of us. To Paul He was very near, for Christ had brought the Everlasting God within reach of man. Through this Jesus, the man of faith could return, by way of repentance, into the very presence of God. And, be sure that whatever journey your minds may take in the economic and political theories of this age, if your hearts take the

road back to God you have made the most notable journey of all. And, in so doing, you have
given God one more bridgehead here on the
shores of time. There is no other hope for you
and me singly as men. There is no other hope
for us collectively as a world.

Jesus, the Resurrected

> *And the angel answered and said unto the women, Fear not ye: for I know that ye seek Jesus, which was crucified. He is not here: for he is risen, as he said.*
> MATTHEW 28:5-6

Resurrection is more than coming back from the dead. Lazarus came back, as did Jairus' daughter and the boy in Nain. Even the apostles brought Tabitha back from death. History records only one *resurrection* from the dead.

Lazarus returned to a life which still had pain and sorrow and at last had to end in death. Not so Christ. He arose from the dead, lives and reigns to all eternity.

Many of you have wished for some dear one to return. But would you really want the dead to return to another round with pain and anguish and death? If that were the only sort of return you could get, would you have the sheer selfishness to ask it?

Christ has promised that as He is risen, so shall we arise. We shall be like Him. At first thought you might envisage that kind of reappearing as a vague, unreal prospect. Better that a person return as the solid, flesh-and-blood person whom you have seen and touched and caressed. All this talk about some distant resurrection leaves you unmoved. Let a man sit up from his bed of death and talk to you again. Anything other or more than that sounds like a fairy tale.

What if the disciples, John and James and Peter, had gotten no more than that on Easter morning. If Jesus had returned, only again to be pursued by His enemies, again to be tried and again to be crucified, and what if that had recurred a dozen times, what note of triumph could the followers of Christ possibly have gotten from such a repeating drama? Jesus arose, solid and real as before, to talk with them and eat with them as before. But there was an eternity of difference. The limitations of this earth, its pain and disease and death, could no longer touch Him. His body was the resurrected body. Far from being less real than it had been, it now was infinitely more solid and real. No power could dissolve it again. The cancerous germ of death and decay was gone. It was a *heavenly body,* a body still, and not some spirit-wisp of cloud. Indeed, it was a glorified body!

The resurrection of Jesus from the dead, and His promise that we shall share it one day, are the crowning chapter of God's story. The death on the cross overcame the enemy, but if there had been no resurrection it would be as if the enemy were still left to occupy and rule. What nonsense would it not have been if after the battle of Waterloo Napoleon had been left to occupy and rule Europe, or if after the final campaign in Germany the victors had retired and left Hitler and his party to occupy and rule Europe as before? The story of Christ and His triumph at Calvary would be left hanging in air were death to have remained unmolested as the field marshal. On Easter morning death, the last enemy, was routed and dispossessed. The devil was not allowed to keep even a vestige of conquest. Even the bodies of men were no longer his, to moulder in graves. In the resurrection of the body of Jesus, the conquering Christ, we have the wondrous promise that these bodies of ours, under the temporary occupation of death, will one day slough off this alien rule and rise again to the fullness of celestial life.

When in the hour of death you stand at the unmoving side of your beloved reluctant to surrender the last fond gaze at the form that short days before had given you warm and loving touch, remember that this attachment you have for a house of clay is not something melancholy and morbid. This body is important, not only because of what it has been but also because of what one day it again shall be. It will rise again.

You will feel its touch again, hear the cadences of its voice again, see the warmth in those eyes again. This prospect is yours because Jesus arose from the dead. Without this faith we are, in Paul's words, of all men most pitiable.

At this point our native sentimentality may rob us of the majestic sweep of this vision. The glory of the resurrection Kingdom will not necessarily reconstruct all the fond attachments of this life. A Romeo and Juliet may not recapture in heaven the ardor of their earthly passions. When the apostle says, "Beloved, now are we the sons of God, and it doth not yet appear what we shall be," he holds forth the promise in heaven of something so incredibly wonderful that earthly forms left behind will not be missed. C. S. Lewis, in making this point, describes a four-year-old boy observing two lovers who are sitting on a davenport eating chocolate candy. To the boy the secret of the lovers' happiness lies in the fact that they have candy. To the lovers the candy is quite incidental to their joy; it could be there, or not, it would make little difference. Similarly, declares Mr. Lewis, we earth-bound creatures are unable to comprehend the essence that makes heaven a place of bliss. Things and relationships which we think very necessary to make heaven meaningful may not be necessary at all. The Lord said, "Behold, I make all things new," and let us allow our Lord to determine the patterns of

the celestial life which shall fill our cup to over-
flowing forevermore. Heaven is not merely an
endless repitition of the loves and ecstasies of
earth, nor does the resurrection usher our bodies
into eternal cycles of birth and hunger and pleasure and pain and death.

To each believer, the resurrection of Jesus
from the dead means primarily the guarantee of
all the wonderful promises that He made. He
had told His disciples, "I have overcome the
world," "I am the door; by me if any man enter
he shall be saved . . .," "I am the way, the truth
and the life," "In my father's house are many
mansions; I go to prepare a place for you . . . ."

These, and many other staggering promises,
had made the hopes and faith of these people
soar to dazzling heights. Friday, at the ninth
hour, their hopes came tumbling down like a
house of sticks. Discouraged and bewildered, they
idled away the long Sabbath hours awaiting Sunday's dawn so that they might do the last, sad
offices for the dead. With the first rays of the sun
they made their sorrowing way to the tomb. What
they saw and heard sent their minds reeling. "He
is not here . . . He is risen" were the cryptic
words of the angel. Mary Magdalene saw Him
that morning. In the afternoon two men talked
with Him on the way to Emmaus; and in the
evening He appeared to several while they were
eating. In the following weeks, He went in and

out among them, much as before, except for a strange and electric difference. It was the same Jesus, yet not the same. It was the same body, yet mysteriously different.

Not until after His ascension and after the outpouring of the Holy Ghost at Pentecost did the full importance of the events burst in upon them. Now they knew. This Jesus had been, and was, the living God. The divine Savior, the Messiah, long promised, had come and gone. But, in coming, He had died for them and for the whole world; and, in leaving, He had promised them a continuing though invisible companionship; and He had crowned His going with the sure promise that He would come again.

The earth on which they still walked and lived was real, to be sure; but the unseen Kingdom of their resurrected Lord was even more real. There could be no doubt of that, because had they not seen Him and touched Him? Had He not eaten with them and spoken to them? This was no dream walking. He was a real Being, with a body more real than theirs, for His was a body with the sting of death forever removed.

He goes on before us, this Jesus, and in faith we follow. And we know that because He, our Redeemer, lives, we too shall live.

Nor do we live only in the prospect of one day inheriting the resurrection of our Lord. In the present moment, while yet encumbered with

this dying body in a world of death, we walk in
a Kingdom that daily keeps defying death. The
image of God which sin and death debauched in
us is revived. We become new creatures, through
faith. Faculties for Christlike living come alive
again. A love which was wholly foreign to our
fallen natures is reborn in our souls. Restored
to God, we become alien to the sinful world
formerly so native to us. We become strangers,
a peculiar people, a colony of Christ's Kingdom
in this world of time.

Although possessed still of our old Adam, the
sinful man of the fallen order, simultaneously we
become new creatures in Jesus Christ, the resurrected Lord. And while we linger about for a
few years awaiting our final adoption, we busy
ourselves untiringly on this far planet with the
throbbing tasks of the eternal Kingdom. We work
without fear and frustration, for we know that
already we have set foot within the borders of
that Kingdom into which on the day of the resurrection we shall be plunged in glory.

Where Will You Station Yourself?

> *But Thomas was not with them when Jesus came. The other disciples therefore said unto him, We have seen the Lord. But he said unto them, Except I shall see in his hands the print of the nails, and put my finger into the print of the nails, and thrust my hand into his side, I will not believe. And after eight days again his disciples were within, and Thomas with them: then came Jesus, the doors being shut, and stood in the midst, and said, Peace be unto you. . .*
> JOHN 20:24-26

Often a man finds it hardest to believe that which he most eagerly wants to believe. If you care very much for someone or something, doubts may crowd in like locusts. Who is more tormented than a lover who cries, "It can't be possible that she loves me." A mother whose son is reported safe and returning from the field of battle will say, "I cannot believe it till I hold him in my arms."

It was that way with Thomas, called Didymus. The others said, "We have seen the Lord." Thomas said, "Except I see in his hands the print of the nails . . . I will not believe." Thomas was no cynic; he was an ardent lover and follower. It was he who had once proposed to the band of disciples that they all follow Jesus to Bethany and Jerusalem even if it meant death for all of them. The tragedy for Thomas was not his lack of love or faithfulness; the pity for this good man was that for eight days he lived in the anguish of uncertainty and doubt. And the reason he failed to have his Easter hopes realized was simply that he had stationed himself in a place other than the place where Jesus appeared. The disciples were together, and Thomas was not with them.

I should like today to suggest a very plain and simple truth: what happens to you in most instances is determined by where you station yourself.

Today you have stationed yourself in these church pews, and for the moment you are in the path of this sermon. I do not know what this sermon may do to you or for you. I think we preachers are the first to wonder whether we have failed the opportunities of the hour. But if the next twenty minutes seem to do nothing for you, do not dismiss the hour as uneventful. Your decision last night or this morning to attend church was the first movement in your experience of worship. You put your foot on the path of God when you crossed your threshold this morning. Through the hymns, confession of sin, the Kyrie, the Gloria, the ancient prayers of the people of God, the confession of faith and the offering of gifts, you already have been in the presence of God. What this hour may have already deposited in the inner recesses of your soul of comfort, faith and strength you may never know. The important thing is that you have this day put yourself in the pathway of God's Word, and the ways of God with the heart of a man are as unpredictable as they are glorious.

The supreme issue in life for each of us is whether or not we have been touched by the Lord, not just brushed with a casual caress like the summer breeze on your brow, but pierced through by the arrow or sword of God. That God may encounter you with His magnetic, decisive and transforming presence is the goal of supreme significance for you and for every man. Life may touch you with many of its variables, wealth or poverty, health or illness, fame or obscurity. These circumstances may come and go, but if your life is decisively pierced by God, all other conditions notwithstanding, your life will have strange and wondrous fulfillment.

It would be sheer presumption for me or for anyone else so to fix God's whereabouts that in

five easy lessons you would surely find Him. He
has clothed Himself in mystery, and He is truly
a "hidden" God. When Nicodemus tried to pin
down the Lord to some sort of fixed process by
which he might enter eternal life, the Lord coun-
tered with what is one of the most beautiful
and wistful passages in all the Bible, "The wind
bloweth where it listeth, and thou hearest the
sound thereof, but canst not tell whence it
cometh, and whither it goeth: so is every one
that is born of the Spirit."

There are three places, however, where, if you
are faithfully stationed, you will have every right
to expect the Lord to appear and make His imprint on your life.

First, in His Word and Sacraments.

Second, within the fellowship of believers or
His Church.

Third, in the company of the world's needy.

While it is true that the Lord moves in all fine
literature, all sublime music and in all great
sculpture and painting, He has chosen to reveal
Himself peculiarly in one Book, and in two visible Sacraments. And while "the invisble things
of him from the creation of the world are clearly
seen, being understood by the things that are
made," without the clear witness of His own
Word we would be left with but an awesome and
comfortless God.

It is in His Word that we encounter Him, the

Word in words, phrases, paragraphs, commas and semicolons, and the Word in water, bread and wine. To deal with this Word as something sacred and absolute apart from its "vessel" of rhetoric and visible elements is to make scholastic and meaningless distinctions on the one hand, and to plunge ourselves into impossible dialectics on the other. With the naivete, or simple trust, of a child, let us station ourselves in the midst of this Word with believing and expectant hearts, and wait for the exciting appearance of our God.

The Bible is the record of a Saving God. It is history, not primarily the story of man's dealings with man, but the chronicle of God's mighty dealings with man. Like a window, it is the vista down which God travels in His redeeming advent to man. Here we have the whole rounded account of the creation, redemption, sanctification and the final prospect of glory which God has enacted for man. And striding through the whole is the figure of Jesus, the Son of God, invading our little planet for our salvation.

Secondly, you encounter Him when you station yourself within the Christian fellowship, or the Church. While we distinguish between the organized, visible Church in congregations and denominations on the one hand and the universal, invisible Church on the other, there is a vibrant fellowship to be found within the congregation which is a foretaste of the society which

shall be ours in heaven. Jesus has promised that
where even two or three are gathered together
in His Name, there He will be in their midst.
And in the concourse of believers, where joys
and sorrows are shared on the level of a common
faith, there one has the right to believe that
Christ will appear. If you truly want to meet Him,
most surely you will not neglect the assembling
together with other seekers and believers.

You cannot come to rest within this fellowship,
however, and think to stay there in sweet pos-
session of the Lord. There is something danger-
ously limiting in the verse,

> Blest be the tie that binds
> Our hearts in Christian love,
> The fellowship of kindred minds
> Is like to that above.

You dare not with God "build a sweet, little nest
somewhere in the west and let the rest of the
world go by." For the Christ also appears in the
thick of the world's needy, whether they chance
to be of kindred or of hostile mind. It is in the
seething cauldron of the earth's hunger and disease, hatred and fear, that Christ appears with
peculiar incarnation. While Jesus surely is em-
bodied in the life of a kind and loving saint, He
has declared that He will parade before you in
the form of the twisted, beaten and disfigured
host of mankind's needy. If you withdraw from

the snarling market place you may fail to find Him in the vaulting temple. For the Lord you find in serene worship on Sunday you must seek in the cries of the hungering on Monday.

Christ walked the earth nineteen hundred years ago in the form of a Galilean peasant. He will reappear on the last day in the royal splendor of the everlasting King. Between these two open appearances, He keeps reappearing in the persons of the people of need. The glory of the Church lies not alone in its memory of Bethlehem and Calvary, nor in its flaming hope of His second coming, but in its daily search of Him in the swirling mass of the world's needy. Failing to station ourselves there, we shall betray both His memory and His final coming in glory.

Most of you have strong impulses to kindness and mercy. These single impulses ought to be made a part of a magnificent faith and mission. You have been created in God's image; you have been reclaimed to the company of heaven by Christ's mighty act of redemption. In that redemption you are given the high portfolio of loving service. Every small and concrete opportunity for kindness becomes the occasion for you, a royal ambassador of the heavenly kingdom, to act for the King. To give a cup of cold water becomes a regal act. Whatever you do in love to the least of men you do for Him and to Him. The little refrain of your charities becomes a phrase in the magnificent symphony of the seven heavens.

Do you want to meet the Lord and know Him? If you do, most assuredly you will seek Him in His Word and Sacraments, the means He Himself has chosen to convey Himself to you. Nor will you disdain the fellowship in His Church. And if you are really in earnest about wanting to find Him, you will plunge into the teeming scene of hungering, blundering, suffering mankind. Station yourself in these three places, and the great, good Lord will not pass you by.

This Incredible Tale

> *If ye then be risen with Christ, seek those things which are above, where Christ sitteth on the right hand of God. Set your affection on things above, not on things on the earth. For ye are dead, and your life is hid with Christ in God. When Christ, who is our life, shall appear, then shall ye also appear with him in glory.* COLOSSIANS 3:1-4

I wish it were possible for me so to preach this word of God from Colossians that you would leave the church today with your minds reeling and spinning. You should be shaking your heads incredulously and saying to yourselves, "Am I really such an amazing creature? Has the great God actually gone to such lengths in planning for me?"

Several times Jesus is recorded as saying sadly to His diciples, "O ye of little faith." Our minds are so riveted to the trivial and confining dimensions of earth, so fearful of setting themselves on things that are above, that we keep on tying our

75

shoestrings when all the heavens are ablaze with meteors and stars.

We confess together the Apostles' Creed. Suppose someone had the audacity to paraphrase the words of the confession, substitute "I" for "Christ," and say—"I was conceived and born . . . I suffered . . . I died . . . I arose from the dead . . . I am at God's side . . . I will one day appear full in glory." What sort of megalomania would you think had struck him?

Essentially that is what Paul is saying has happened to you. You died, you were raised with Christ, your life is hidden for the moment in His; and when He again appears, in the very same event you, who are hidden in Him, will appear in glory.

What tripe, or madness, is this? If you have the twin gifts of imagination and faith, prepare to use them. For this is the Gospel, the glorious good news of man being swallowed up in a salvation and a glory not his own. It is far more intelligible to be speaking about the traditional subjects of righteousness, justice, charity and patience. But these are *fruits* of the Spirit, the visible results of being swept up and overcome by the Spirit of God. Most of you can navigate intelligibly among the great moral precepts and still keep your wheels on the ground. The Gospel sweeps you up into the celestial stratosphere, into inter-planetary flights. The tragedy is that we who might take off with God into the limitless spaces of His domain use up all our spiritual gasoline taxiing along the ground. And we wonder why we do not see anything breathtaking.

You have been raised with Christ, the Apostle declares. But somewhere along the line you must then have died. How can you have died, if now you are alive and listening to Paul? Obviously, the "you" which Paul singles out is not the "you" who eats and sleeps, writes with a pen, marries and has children. He is speaking of the "natural self," the "you" who by birth has inherited the fallen nature and order of Adam. This "you" must die. By nature you are a person of caprice, a lawless self, a ball tossed hither and yon by the whims of passion and circumstance. By nature you are a person of competition, a struggling and fighting self concerned primarily with the pride of pre-eminence and prestige. This capricious and competitive self must die.

This "you" begins to die with the first stroke of God's law. In his letter to the Romans, Paul describes the happy lawlessness of the self who has not yet confronted the law of God. He says, " . . . if it had not been for the law, I should not have known sin. I should not have known what it is to covet if the law had not said, 'Thou shalt not covet' . . . Apart from the law sin lies dead. I was once alive apart from the law, but when the commandment came, sin revived *and I died.*"

Thousands of people live apart from this law of God. The course of their lives may be sufficiently hedged in by customs, traditions and the normal inhibitions of the world around them so that they escape prison. They live a life quite unregulated by the inner moral law of God, however regimented they may be by the rules of environment. They are decent, proper and nice. But they are dead to the whole universe of God's law, and live the heedless life of a well-conditioned animal. But the moment they stick their noses within the domain of God's holy law, this "animal life" begins to suffocate. For no human animal can inherit the Kingdom of God.

If at this point a man will make the decision to try living between God's poles of right and wrong, he is definitely on the way to having one "self" die and another "self" be born. He must try. Using all the imagined powers of his will, he must try to fulfill the high law of God's holiness. But however gallantly he may try, he keeps sinking deeper and deeper into the death that yawns to swallow him. With Paul, he will cry, "The good that I would I do not; but the evil which I would not, that I do. O wretched man that I am! who shall deliver me from the body of this death?" It is when this man, the moral man, the man who is trying with might and main to fulfill God's law—it is when this man finally capitulates to his own total incompetence that the great chariot of the Gospel swoops down to pick him up. When the struggling one ceases at last to struggle, Jesus takes him into His arms. When the night of total despair at last swallows him up, the day of total grace dawns.

Nothing short of the Holy Spirit Himself can bring us to the brink of this self-abasement. Each of us is inclined to rely again and again on our own moral achievements to justify the demands of God's law. Yet, sin leaves nothing untainted; its lurid mark besmears every thought and deed. Kant has said, "There is something in the misfortune of our best friends which does not displease us." However compassionate we may try to become, we can read about millions of starving people and sit down to our own lavish tables with undisturbed and lusty appetites. We hear the call to love, but a deep-seated indifference paralyzes us. We are birds that struggle to fly but have no wings. We have an impulse to rise up and walk, but we have no legs. We hear the call to singleness of purpose, and are distracted by the chaos of our urges, inclinations and impulses. Paul said that the law of sin which dwelt in his members made him captive to sin. Such is the despair of the person who struggles to square himself with the law of God.

Despair and grace are the twin-therapy of God.

Grace strikes when despair has laid low all of man's pretended defenses. Grace strikes when we walk in the dark valley of meaninglessness and empty life. It strikes when we are in great pain and restlessness. It strikes when our disgust for our own being, our indifference, our weakness, our hostility, our lack of direction and composure have become intolerable to us. When year after year the longed-for perfections of life do not appear, when the old compulsions reign within us as they have for decades, when despair destroys all joy and courage—then grace strikes!

The incredible message of grace is that you are accepted. Despite anything you are or have done or have failed to do, you are accepted. In and through Christ, your Brother-Savior, you are accepted by your Heavenly Father. That which is greater than you enfolds you. Do not try to do anything now; perhaps later you will do much. Do not seek for anything, do not perform anything, do not intend anything. Simply rest back in the glorious fact that you are accepted. Let the eternal moment of grace sink in upon your troubled heart. You are loved; you are cradled in the everlasting arms. You are swallowed up, and your life is hid in Christ. That is grace!

Your old capricious and competitive self is in death throes, and a new life is born. Nothing in all God's universe is as momentous as this event in you. The death of one civilization and the emergence of a new is but a casual event compared with the new birth in you. You, and not civilizations, are eternal. The rise and fall of nations, the shifting of river beds, the ordering of planets, suns and stars in their orbits are but the daily chores of our God. That which excites Him is what happens to you—an eternal soul. He did not die to create new heavens; He died on a cross to capture you.

Only once in my memory has the fate of one person captured the imagination of the world, and for an hour crowded out all else. At twenty-four minutes after ten on the night of May 21, 1927, over the airport of Paris there slipped out of the darkness a gray-white airplane and lighted on the far side of the field as a hundred thousand people pressed forward to welcome the first man to fly alone across the Atlantic from New York to Paris. That afternoon the *New York Times* was flooded with ten thousand telephone calls of inquiry. The *Times* for May 22nd reports, "New York bubbled all day yesterday with excitement and expectancy, first yearning for word of Captain Lindbergh, then half-doubting, gaining confidence as the afternoon progressed, finally acclaiming victory in the greatest demonstration the western world had seen for a decade . . . ," all because of a boyish looking man whose fate was undetermined until his craft came to rest in a firm place.

Your flight has heaven all astir. God and the legions of angels are observing you with bated breath, hoping you will come to rest on the firm rock of your salvation, restless until your life is hid with Christ in God—until you rest back in the wondrous fact of grace. When you at last accept the amazing truth that you are accepted —you, the indifferent, the fainthearted, the bewildered and fretful, the rebellious and sinful one—when you echo from your heart,

> Just as I am, without one plea,
> But that Thy blood was shed for me,
> And that Thou bid'st me come to Thee,
> O Lamb of God, I come!

then all heaven will burst forth in peans of joy and hallelujahs.

Molested by the Vanquished

> *A little while and ye shall not see me: and again, a little while, and ye shall see me, because I go to the Father . . . Verily, verily I say unto you, That ye shall weep and lament, but the world shall rejoice, and ye shall be sorrowful, but your sorrow shall be turned into joy.*
>
> JOHN 16:16, 20

When at the end of the last war Germany was defeated, there were one million Nazi troops in Norway. These forces could easily have held out for a time against the small country.

Let us suppose that they had elected to continue their dominion. Then Norway, a part of the victorious Allies, would have been ruled by the defeated enemy. The victors would have been ruled by the vanquished. And though victors, they would have been suffering discomforts, buffetings and persecutions at the hands of a power which already was defeated and undone.

Such is somewhat the situation on our planet.

The central forces of Satan were overcome and conquered nineteen hundred years ago. Christ emerged the victor in the decisive battle for this world. And in this interval of centuries that has followed, while we await the final cleaning-up action, the people of God find themselves in the strange situation of being molested, enticed, threatened, persecuted and sometimes crushed by a defeated power.

In such a situation how is a child of God to find happiness? How is he to achieve "peace of mind"? Jesus gives us a clue, ". . . ye shall weep and lament . . . ye shall be sorrowful, but your sorrow shall be turned to joy . . . be of good cheer, I have overcome the world."

Had this situation prevailed in Norway, a citizen would face the choice of two kinds of peace or happiness. He could collaborate with the enemy, come to terms with the occupying power, and be spared the tensions and collisions that might torment his life. Or, he could remain an adamant patriot, faithful to his suffering country, and have the inner peace of an uncompromised conscience. During the war, when the Nazi troops were in full occupation, the Norwegian primate, Berggrav, declared that the only place a patriot could really be happy was in jail. Out of jail, he could only live with the unhappy fear that his life had not been worthy enough to merit the enemy's punishment.

We are not altogether realistic when we tell ourselves that if we are decent, fair, industrious, honest and God-fearing, we will prosper. That would be true if in this world the forces that dislike honesty, integrity, righteousness and purity were already annihilated or were so emasculated that they could not give vigorous protest. To say glibly that this is God's world and that if we go God's way we shall surely be rewarded is to ignore the stubborn fact that we live in a fallen world.

There are enemies afoot. This is not a nice world where nice people have a nice time. Powerful forces are pitted against the Kingdom of God and its people. The utmost vigilance and wisdom are required. Every moment we must watch and pray that we be not undone. And there are times in the history of men, or of a man, when the forces of evil, though defeated, are leagued into singular fierceness. There are hours when the victors, those who in faith have been given Christ's victory, will weep and lament. The strife will seem more than they can bear.

The enemy is a vanquished foe, but the Scriptures point to three sectors on which we still wage battle. We fight against the devil and his hosts, against a world in which evil is often an organized social force, and against the deep inclinations to sin in our own natures. It is not enough to say that every man struggles against and within his environment for survival, for survival is not the real prize. Eternal life is the military objective for every child of God, and to attain this goal more is required than an adeptness for survival.

Twentieth century man, until very recently, had dismissed the devil as an amusing legend. The fury of destruction unleashed in rising tyrannies and a second world war has in part returned the devil to his old prestige. But we still fail to give him his dramatic due in the strife.

Any realistic reading of the Scriptures most certainly must convince us that the devil is treated as more than a myth. In the Bible he is a very real being. Remember how he entered into King Saul and ruined a good ruler, making him a victim of pride, envy, suspicion, self-pity and vindictiveness. Again and again Jesus is reported to have cast out demons. For Luther, who speaks of the ancient foe still out to work us woe, Satan was no poetic fiction. The grim bargain of Goethe's Dr. Faustus with Mephistopheles may be a literary device, but it was written for an age that took the devil seriously. Nor are we altogether without our modern voices. C. S. Lewis, among others, has reintroduced the dramatic character of this enemy in his *Screwtape Letters* and many of his other works.

For every child of God Satan is a real foe. We sense the solemn truth of Paul's warning that "we wrestle not against flesh and blood." Actually, it

is a lack of implicit faith in the Word of God or a
lack of imagination, or both, which tempt us to
dismiss the devil from the field of battle. Certainly it is dialectical nonsense to believe in God
as a personal Being and refuse to believe in the
possibility of a rival being.

The tragic consequence of overlooking the
devil is the loss of vital prayer. If the enemy is
not from without, why seek help from without?
If our ills arise from a maladjusted environment
and a shoddy heredity, we can cope with the
situation through social engineers and psychia-
trists.

Napoleon once said, "He who would be victor
must know his enemy." Mankind will blunder in
his over-all strategy and become easy prey unless
he recovers a profound respect and fear of the
devil as "a roaring lion seeking whom he may
devour."

The second sector defined by Scripture is the
world. Wicked men and wicked structures or
organizations among men make up a hostile world.
In every age the climate of life, politically and
economically, ideologically and culturally, may
have elements arrayed against the Kingdom of
God. Reinhold Niebuhr's title, *Moral Man in
Immoral Society,* states the plight of individual
man as he moves in and out in society. Some
periods of the world's history offer more congenial
climate than others, but in every age the problem

rears its ugly head. The noblest efforts of men seem often to be cancelled out by an evil which twists and distorts his corporate life into ruthless and destructive ends. He hates war, but world movements sweep him into war. He seeks security and survival, and his cooperative striving yields tyranny and slavery. All the world can complain in the words of Paul, " . . . the good I would I do not, the evil I would not that I do."

Perhaps not since the first centuries of the Christian era has the Church found itself in as hostile a world climate as in the middle twentieth century. This is a new day of martyrdom. From the time Constantine made Christianity the faith of the court, the Western World has witnessed an almost continuous alliance between civil rulers and the ecclesiastical powers; this century has witnessed a rift between them, and in Europe a state of open defiance. The Church's right to teach the Gospel and to engage in organized charities is openly challenged by the rising welfare states in many areas. The enemy seems to have strengthened his forces in *the World*. And Christians, who are in the world but not of the world, find themselves under new imperatives to oppose and transform the world.

The self, who by birth has inherited the fearful drag of the Fall, constitutes the third salient in the battle against the foe. God establishes a new life within a person whenever He is given the opportunity through His means of grace, the Word and the Sacraments. This new life lives side by side with man's sinful endowment in the tension of a fearful dualism. Every Christian, therefore, has a self to be resisted and a self to be honored. In a continuous round, sometimes called the daily renewal, we subdue the evil self, the Old Adam, and seek to empower the good self, or the New Man. This New Man is actually Christ living within us, and although in His strength we need no longer be under the domination of sin, until the end we shall have to move toward the crown in fear and trembling.

You were created to be heirs of God; you were redeemed to become soldiers of the cross. You do have the option, however, of surrendering your birthright, denying your destiny, and capitulating to the enemy. You may live at peace with Satan, the sinful world and your own fallen self. At best it will be the uneasy and awesome peace of a bit of debris floating willy-nilly down the rapids of unrestrained passion, ambition and pleasure. To pit yourself against the stream will add conflict to your outward life, but pitting yourself against the enemy will make you eligible for the peace of God—that inner peace—which the world cannot give, and which passeth understanding. You will be able to live with yourself, not because you smack your lips with Little Jack Horner and say "what a good boy am I," but because your sins and failures are swallowed up daily by the infinite forgiveness which is in Christ. You will walk in courage and tranquility, in the very midst of the conflict, because through faith the victory of Christ has become your victory. You may be, and will be, molested your life through by the devil, the world, and your sinful self, but you are not the vanquished. You are the victors!

Heirs of What?

> *For ye have not received the spirit of bondage again to fear; but ye have received the Spirit of adoption, whereby we cry, Abba Father. The Spirit itself beareth witness with our spirit, that we are the children of God: And if children, then heirs; heirs of God, and joint-heirs with Christ; if so be that we suffer with him, that we may be also glorified together.* ROMANS 8:15-17

Alexander the Great, at twenty-nine, grieved because there were no more worlds to conquer, and a year later died from his own boredom.

It is a mood not unlike that of Alexander that hangs over our twentieth century. If you are to muster some gallantry and speak of new frontiers to conquer, to most of the world you may seem very much like frightened children whistling in the dark. After all, both north and south poles have been explored, the seven seas are long since spanned, the air lanes have been mastered, and the infinitesimal atom has been abducted. What can there be left to capture?

Before you sally forth in search of new worlds to conquer, I beg of you to take sober stock of what you have to work with. The middle twentieth century calls for some realistic appraisal. After all, it would be silly of you to pay an entrance fee to run the decathlon if you are a paralytic. Why attempt to fly if you have no wings? It may be romantic and gallant to seek the gold at the end of the rainbow, but it is foolhardy at best if there is no pot of gold there.

For better or for worse, you come to this hour of history having inherited a given set of equipment and circumstances.

Because you are men, and not angels, you are heirs of a fallen nature and a fallen world order. You may feel like a Sir Galahad, and all the trumpets of your being may sound forth for advance, but the fact remains that you ride a very perverse steed, and your world is filled with more dragons than you know. Nor is this a current situation in history. In the long story of the race, from the time of Adam's fall, the way has been beset by forces that have dogged every human effort to good. You, yourself, have within you the drag of a nature deeply prejudiced for evil and disinclined toward good. Whatever change the political and economic face of the world may make at any given period of history, the nature of man remains perennially the same. Unless a rival nature is bestowed from without, by God, man himself remains a helpless victim in a world of change.

Moreover, you come to this hour in history the heir of fallen faiths. That which braced up the courage of our grandfathers is largely gone. We have been disillusioned from former naive faiths in the goodness of human nature, the inevitable spiral of progress, the sure victory of democracy, and the illimitable resources of technology. It is hard to let these faiths go, and much of the world is prostrate in a strangling cynicism. If the warm promises of these hopes have turned cold, why rally to anything?

Even in the gloom of fallen faiths there is light, however, if the faiths that have fallen were false. Honest despair is firmer ground than burlesque optimism. You cannot build on a mirage, nor can you find your way following a phantom. Perhaps the most promising symptom of this dark hour is the bankruptcy of false faiths. Having ceased our chase of fireflies, we may look for the stars.

But there are new will-o'-the-wisps. You are heirs of new illusions. From psychoanalysis to social planning, a whole army of new candidates for your hope has invaded the scene. If life is too much for you and you collapse in frustration, let a psychiatrist dig around in your soul and induce peace. If a rampant nationalism threatens to bring the whole world tumbling down around you, get on the bandwagon for internationalism.

Or, if all prospects fail, why not plunge into life with an animal abandon and for the brief present eat, drink and be merry in whatever grim manner you may?

It is enough to make you stop before you ever begin—if you add up the odds against you in this matter of conquest. If you, yourself, are made of such frail stuff, and if you confront a world filled with such hostility, why try at all?

You would most certainly throw in the sponge were it not for one other towering fact: *you are heirs of God!* That one fact alone recasts this whole matter of existence. If you were a pauper begging alms from an insolvent world, you could quit; but you are a prince sent to earth on a most significant planetary assignment. Your rank, your resources and your mission are all derived from heaven; they do not stem from earth at all. Your birth into this fallen world makes you heirs of a sorry age, but your rebirth into sonship with God reopens the limitless power of the eternal for you.

This titanic turn of events for you occurred at a suburban spot outside of Jerusalem over nineteen hundred years ago. There the only begotten Son of God died on a cross for the explicit purpose of winning your right to be a son of God. How this could be, your little mind will never be able to comprehend. But let your heart embrace this strange and wondrous event, and all the events of your life will take on new color. At Golgotha, the Almighty God in Christ did something which instantly changed your total status. Nineteen hundred years before your birth God already had provided you with rights to a standing of perfect righteousness; long before you were a being at all, He had made provision for the forgiveness of all your sins. All this Jesus did for you, before your grandfather was born. His redemptive act at Calvary opened the doors for your free passage into the royal house of God, and entitled you to share with Christ the inheritance of God, the angels and the saints. You who had become slaves in Adam's fall had become sons in Christ's death.

The privilege and power to renounce this divine right still remained yours, however. In indifference or rebellion, you can escape a prince's inheritance. But if you do not have an heir's riches, it will be because you have neglected in faith to receive it. The fault will be yours, and in your poverty and misery you need not cry to high heaven about the injustices of your lot. You have been elected to sonship. You are an heir, with all the rights of an heir. God has seen to that.

Moreover, He keeps calling to you in Word and Sacrament. The Holy Spirit broods over you. In numberless ways He prods you to yield your self-will and return to the Father's house.

To be an heir of God! What gigantic propor-

tions life may have for you! Think of the power
at your command! You take inventory of your
frail assets, and every task seems impossible of
achievement. But take stock of the assets of God
—now at your disposal as an heir of God—and
nothing seems impossible. To every prospect and
to every situation, you bring the cumulative resources of God. The Standard Oil Company, for
instance, has vast power. If it chooses, the company
may concentrate its credits and resources upon
any given local situation in its immense chain of
holdings. To you, one heir of heaven, heaven can
release the full power of its infinite resources for
any given problem. The fullness of God can be
yours; you need never again settle for a tiny
fraction of the Lord's forgiveness, comfort or
strength. You have the right to expect that you
may command the unpredictable wonders of the
Kingdom of God in what may seem a trifling
incident. You live not in your own strength, but
in the boundless power of God.

As heirs, you are drawn into the incredible
dimensions of the heavenly kingdom. Your life
upon earth is no longer a mere struggle for survival; now it becomes an adventure in the Kingdom. The dealings of your trade are now, in
Jacob Marley's words, ". . . but a drop in the
comprehensive ocean of my business." Your
affairs are Christ's program for the world, your
aspirations are Christ's divine dreams for men,

your anguish is now the yearning of the heart of
Christ. Threatened by life's pettiness and fears,
in faith you are lifted to the high plateaus from
which you catch sight of the everlasting hills. The
winds may blow more fierce, it is true, but up
there on the tablelands of the Kingdom you walk
amid the stars of light. As the forgiven one, your
task is to forgive; as the one to whom mercy has
been given, you are to bestow mercy; as the empowered one, you are to walk in power. Now a
prince in the house of God, a fellow-heir with
Christ, you are to take captive for Him every area
of this planet's life. You cannot in mournful piety
abdicate your princely station in economics, politics, science or art. All is Christ's and you are to
have dominion for Him. In this battle for conquest the frontiers are ever new.

To be sure, you will suffer. But you will suffer
as a prince. And the suffering will itself be your
glory, the glory you share with the Suffering Lord.
And one day, the din of earth's battles forever
stilled and earth's sufferings forever over, you will
share with Him the glory that shall never end.

Why Did They Die?

> *And fear not them which kill the body,
> but are not able to kill the soul: but
> rather fear him which is able to destroy
> both soul and body in hell.*
> MATTHEW 10:28

Memorial Day is here again. Millions of graves will receive their annual care. The dead, often forgotten during the long year, will be remembered for a moment. There is a sense in which the graves should be forgotten. A person who lives only in the past may grow melancholy and morbid. No one should bury the zest for living and the hopes for the future in some sentimental grave.

On the other hand, there are good reasons for spending much thought with the graves. Man ought to have a past tense. Memories should be precious. The heritage which the fathers gave us should be carried with thankfulness to them. Then, too, we ought not to shy away from the sobering fact that some day we too will rest in some grave. Life is a bird on the wing that has but a little way to flutter. Many of the anxieties and ambitions we guard so passionately would assume their correct proportions and seem trivial if we kept before us the nearness of the grave. Moreover, the bodies that rest in graves have future significance. There will be a resurrection of the dead. The bodies themselves will be torn out of the grip of death and decay to be restored, and to rejoin the soul. The bodies you lay tenderly to rest are precious not alone because of what they have been, but also because of what they yet will be.

While Memorial Day has become the occasion for remembering all the dead, the day originally was set aside to remember the heroic dead of war. The past great war is sufficiently removed now for us to memorialize the dead without the piercing pain which overwhelmed us the first year. There are wives and children and parents whose hearts still bleed. But time has a way of easing the anguish.

With the short perspective that the past several years have given us, let us today survey the task which their death enforces upon us.

The first point I should like to make is that they did not die in order that you might live. Just to live is not enough. Their lives were too great a price to pay just so that you might eat and make love and grow fat. There is no logic in asking a young man to give up his life in order

that an old man might grow rich. Many a father
and mother today will choke back bitter tears,
and wonder if that is all their boy's death has
meant. They would so like to think that the death
of their son has meant more righteousness and
freedom for this old world. And, they have that
right, before God and man. They have a right to
see their nation use freedom of speech to raise
its voice against all injustice and greed. They
have a right to expect the people to use their
freedom of assembly for the purpose of united
defense of all that is true and honorable. They
have a right to a freedom of press that is employed
to publish only in accordance with the highest
ethical standards of the public welfare. They have
a right to see a people use its blood-bought freedom of worship to fill the churches and
to obey God.

In all candor, and with utter shame, we must
confess that for millions of Americans freedom
means simply the opportunity to do what they
jolly well please. That sort of freedom is not
worth one life on Iwo Jima or Bataan. We often
speak in high economic praise of our free enterprise. If that means freedom for any businessman
to charge excessive profits because people are in
great need of his goods, if it means freedom for
a professional man to exact large fees from people
who must have his services, if, in a word, it begins to mean that people think they are free to

take what they can get, then our economic freedom is a new type of economic tyranny. Real freedom dies when the sense of right and wrong, or the sense of fair play is gone. The heart of freedom is ethical and spiritual. If a man, or a nation, does not do freely and voluntarily that which is right, the death of a million men on the field of battle or the enacting of a million laws in the halls of congress will not save freedom. The men whose names we today honor as the heroic dead did not die in order that you might be free to live, and do as you please. They died in order that you might live and freely do what in high duty you ought to do.

A brief survey of our national life cannot give us ease as we face these dead. Immediately after the war we used our freedom to bet a billion and a half in one year on the races; the same year we used our freedom to defeat an appropriation of a hundred million for cancer research. Last year we used our economic freedom to pyramid national earnings to nearly two hundred billions; we also used our freedom to keep the earnings of over half of our families below $125 a month. We have used our freedom to break one home in three, to spend four times as much for liquor as for milk, to multiply crimes against life and property, and to excuse 85 per cent of our people from entering the House of God on the Sabbath.

Let us ask ourselves in all soberness today, as

the silent army of our dead marches before us, what has become of the prayer we sing in our national hymn?

> O beautiful for spacious skies,
> For amber waves of grain . . .
> America! America!
> God mend thine every flaw,
> Confirm thy soul in self-control,
> Thy liberty in law.

There is no liberty except within the eternal laws of justice. There is no freedom outside of the passion for that which is right. Freedom then becomes license, and license is anarchy.

Christ once told His followers, "Fear not them which kill the body, but are not able to kill the soul." In a national sense, our 300,000 dead in the last war gave their bodies as a small price if America would keep her soul. But America is freedom, and the soul of freedom is righteousness and truth.

On every hand today we are invited to fear the rising power of the Eastern World. If Russia is allowed to go on collecting satellites, what may she do to us? There no doubt is a clash of ideologies between our way of life and the political centralization of power in the Soviet party. But for 98 per cent of Americans the fear of Russia has nothing to do with their understanding of political or economic organization. Most of us are merely whipped into excitement over the fear

of someone growing stronger than we. Christ
cautions us not to fear them which kill the body,
so long as we keep our own soul intact. Students
of history have told us that no nation has been
conquered from the outside; they have first fallen
apart on the inside. Immoral living, greed, and
the pursuit of pleasure disorganize and rot the
inner life of a nation, until it has neither the
energy nor the will to protect itself from the outside. Its soul is gone, and without a vibrant and
stalwart soul, no nation lives.

If these war dead should be allowed just one day
to read our current press and hear today's radio,
would they not wonder at our strange excitement
over the Russia whose virtues we so extolled when
they were our war allies? And should these dead
be allowed to speak, I wonder if they would not
bring us up short with an invitation to a new and
different kind of excitement. I believe they would
tell us that whatever judgment God's history
would have for Russia, the matter of supreme
concern for us would be to keep our national
soul. And, in the deepest sense, our national soul
cannot be kept unless you and I turn to the
matters that concern your soul and mine. If we,
one by one, fail, America will fail. No nation in
all history has been as powerful as we are today.
Christ has said that to whom much is given of
him shall much be required. No nation, therefore, has ever had such cause to tremble before

the awful judgment of God's eternal court as we today. As America goes today, so goes the world tomorrow. If in her soul America is not confirmed in self-control, if in her soul America does not exercise her liberty within the law of God, then the freedom and the governments of the world are in peril. As the soul of America goes today, so goes the world tomorrow.

If we shall keep faith today with these honored dead, we ought to seek the doors of a thousand churches to bow in penitence before our God, and to plead with Him for the mercy and wisdom and strength to carry the torch which from the eternities these dead fling to us today.

If You Look Upward

And when he had said these things, as they were looking, he was taken up; and a cloud received him out of their sight. And while they were looking steadfastly into heaven as he went, behold two men stood by them in white apparel; which also said, Ye men of Galilee, why stand ye looking into heaven? This Jesus, which was received up from you into heaven, shall so come in like manner as ye beheld him going into heaven.
ACTS 1:9-11

There are several directions toward which you may fix your gaze, and with varying degrees of profit.

You may look around you. It is not an altogether pleasant panorama. You will see a world of greed, suspicion, envy and fear. Millions of distractions shriek at you from every conceivable advertising and communications medium. A babble of voices fills your ears with noise and din. There is very little around you to give courage and hope.

You may look behind you. A long look at history, with its rise and fall of civilizations, its debt of the past clamoring for payment, its cargo of opportunities missed welling up with a great tide of remorse—this backward look is not at all reassuring

You may look before you. However gallant you try to be about the future, the rolling clouds that bank your vision and block out the tomorrows offer little solace. You may try to squeeze out some comfort in the thought that since you have not encountered disasters in the past you most surely will be spared them in the future. But you are whistling in the dark.

You may look within you. To take refuge within yourself, in a type of psychopathic monasticism, is a popular twentieth century avocation, but hardly a successful one. Socrates confessed that a long look within himself was the most disquieting look of all, because he found there only a monster. No person has really succeeded in "getting away from it all" by the inward look, because you yourself are a composite of past, present and future, with all the environmental and hereditary ills packed into that self of yours.

A world that is glutted with the grim news of contemporary events, a world that probes history for some pattern of value and progress, a world that plans furtively for the future with a fever for vast social dynamics, a world that seeks refuge in new cults of psychology to eke out some peace from the jig-saw jumble of appetites, urges and frustrations—this world has largely forgotten *the upward look*. We are an age that has overlooked the north star and the principles of celestial navigation. Fortunately, I believe, a world that has long been becoming secular and earth-bound is finding such scant hope from its secular outlook that the day for the upward look may be upon us.

On this day of the Lord's ascension, I address you with three questions:

If you are not looking up, why aren't you?

When you do look up, what do you see?

Having looked up, what then are you compelled to do?

We live in a world of distractions. In America it is the distractions of opulence, in much of the world the distractions of sheer want. What time do we have to look up, when almost every home commands a radio, television and an automobile? The art of silence and meditation is largely lost to the American nation. Even an hour of worship on Sunday morning needs to be buttressed with a good concert choir and a scintillating sermon if it is not to fall stale and boresome. The invitation to a moment of silent prayer sends our minds wandering aimlessly over the hemisphere until the pastor's voice breaks the frightening silence and rescues us from the peril of looking up. From morning till night we feed on a fast

moving parade of distractions. It is a sad com-
mentary on the human being that the Lord often
has to wipe the distractions away with sickness or
sorrow or economic want before He can capture
our eye and ear.

Of course, the basic reason we are not looking
up is that we are sinful beings. To look up only
intensifies our sense of guilt, and increases our
discomfort. If you have exceeded the speed limit,
you look around to escape the policeman and not
to find him. If you have offended God's law,
obviously you hope to avoid His gaze and not
encounter it. Before you will fix your gaze upward, God will have to trouble your conscience
enough to make you desire a thorough-going
peace.

If you try looking upward, what do you see?
It takes some real prodding on the part of the
Holy Spirit to make you see Christ, high and
lifted up. Many people look up and with dismay
see only what Omar Khayyam saw,

> And this inverted bowl we call the sky,
> Whereunder, crawling, cooped, we live and die,
> Reach not your hands to it for help,
> For it as impotently moves as you or I.

You cannot come with unbelieving eyes and un-
disciplined life and expect the heavens to open
and reveal their glory. Looking up, perhaps you
see nothing more than the wonder expressed by
your child,

Twinkle, twinkle little star,
How I wonder what you are,
Up above the world so high,
Like a diamond in the sky.

And that is not enough, splendid as it is to have a sense of wonder.

To see Christ filling the skies, you will first have to find Him as the Christ of the Gospel, in God's Word. Within that Word the Holy Spirit opens your eyes to see your own sinfulness and guilt and to see Jesus on a cross for your salvation. It is within that Word that your eyes of faith are focused for the upward look. The vast panorama of the astronomer's heavens is reduced to absurdly simple proportions when Jesus is revealed through the Word to a repentant and believing heart.

Last evening I chanced to hear over the radio the currently popular song, "How much is that dog in the window, the dog with the waggly tail?" Introducing the next song, the announcer said they would sing the all time favorite of children, and over the air came, "Jesus loves me, this I know; for the Bible tells me so." And I was struck with the thought that wherever the love of God has reached the human heart it has come through this simple child-like logic, ". . . for the Bible tells me so." The vast reaches of the starry heights will not whisper the love of God, and looking into its twinkling mass you will fail to be overwhelmed by God's love unless you have first encountered it in God's Good Book.

Let the Scriptures help you, and looking up you see a God who has no idea of letting you down. You look around you and see hostile faces, cruel men, capricious fortunes and impersonal movements all swirling to get you. You look back into history, and you see the appalling debt which the past has dropped at your doorstep—like a farm which your grandfather encumbered with a first mortgage and your father with a second, both of which you must pay off before the farm is yours. You look forward, and see a threatening future rumbling in ominous prospect. You look within you, and see a wild, perverse and lazy self, plunging headlong, heedless of your good interest. But looking up, you see a God who created you and who could not let you go. You see Him send His son to the earth to die for you. You see the Holy Spirit sent to finish in you the work which began at creation, was interrupted by the fall, was restored in the redemption of Christ, and which He intends to complete in Glory. This is the covenant God, the God of the promise. Again and again He would have had every right to be done with us. When Abraham lied and Jacob stole and Moses killed and David committed adultery—He could have called it off. But in the fullness of time He lifted against time's horizons a Cross, the luminous pledge of His eternal love and faithfulness. And it is that Cross which we should see above all else as we lift our eyes upward.

Having looked up like that, you can never be the same again. You cannot leave the memory of that Face on the Cross and go back to a grim chase after this world's distractions. You cannot go looking around and whimper because you do not have Cadillacs and Florida vacations.

You rest back in these great arms that span the heavens from pole to pole, confident that you cannot drift beyond their tender care. You throw yourself into every good work, your hands strengthened for missions of love and your tongue sweetened with words of patience, pardon and praise. And while engaged in the day's teeming opportunities for tasks of eternal consequence, you live daily in the exhilarating and triumphant expectation of His second and final coming and the full victory that He will bestow on that day. Looking up into the strong, smiling face of your Lord, you go on one step at a time into a sure and incredible future.

You Cannot Be a Happy Animal

For as many as are led by the Spirit of God, they are the sons of God. For ye have not received the spirit of bondage again to fear; but ye have received the Spirit of adoption, whereby we cry, Abba, Father. The Spirit itself beareth witness with our spirit, that we are the children of God: and if children, then heirs; heirs of God, and joint-heirs with Christ; if so be that we suffer with him, that we may be also glorified together.

ROMANS 8:14-17

You can have fun as a sinner, and you can have fun as a saint. But, in between, as a reluctant cautious Christian, you will be intolerably bored. And the pity of so much of our discipleship is that we have never gotten over the hump to where we are having fun being Christian. We are like bathers who have left the ease of lounging on the beach to take to the water, but have been wading only up to our ankles or knees, all the while with chattering teeth, looking longingly back to the beach or occasionally gazing a bit wistfully out to the deep where real swimmers and divers are having themselves a rollicking time.

There are Christians who, having left the tents of wickedness, have failed in courage to stride into the palace and join company with the King.

In the Bible it is often said of God's people, ". . . and they were filled with the Holy Ghost," and invariably they were the people who were tasting some new found joy and peace and power. They had thrown caution to the winds, they were caught up in a quiet ecstasy, they had the glint of excitement and adventure in their eye, they had made a clean break with something and they were in clean, certain stride toward something.

Now, why is it that we run-of-the-mill church people are missing so much of that joy? Someone from the outside will say of us, and quite justly so perhaps, that he has no desire to get involved with us who pretend to be better than the open sinners and yet are critical, harsh, unforgiving, glum, humorless, without imagination and without laughter. And he may go on to point out that for all our talk about a great King and a Kingdom, we are as plebeian a crowd as you can find.

Precisely that we are, altogether too often. We envy the sinner his fun and the saint his joy, but as for us we plod along day after day slaves to dull duty. Our consciences keep us from plunging back into the reckless whirl of sin, and our selfish wills frighten us from the leap into gallant discipleship.

There is no doubt about the fact that you can have fun as a sheer animal. With conscience asleep or ignored, you can live in unrestrained abandon to pleasure. You take your fun where you find it—a new dish, a new drink, a new woman —you taste and move on, and no regrets. You follow a sportive Mephistopheles wherever he leads. If it is money you want, you are never bothered by those prudish companions of honesty, fair dealing or sympathy. You come in with both fists flying and have one whale of a time getting a few thousand. If it is power and prestige you want, and you need to hobnob with the questionable pals of cunning, intrigue, deception, flattery or blackmail to get it, who cares as long as you get elected or end up on top of the heap. You see, it can be great, grim fun being a mere animal, for an animal lives without conscience.

You people here today have gotten yourselves in a spot. Since childhood most of you have heard the Gospel, telling you that you are not animals. And because the Gospel is the power of God, it does not leave you untouched, as a legend or a myth would. You can hear about Santa Claus and Snow White and Prince Charming, and go right on being happy animals. But you cannot hear about Jesus Christ without being disturbed, however faintly. When you hear the Gospel you hear a bell calling you away from this animal fun. It is the Holy Spirit calling you away from something and to something. It is like an evening chapel chime, at once full of peace and full of terror. Once you have really heard it, you can never again be a thoroughly happy animal.

The apostle Paul describes this Word's work in his life, "For I was alive without the law once: but when the commandment came, sin revived, and I died. And the commandment, which was ordained to life, I found to be unto death." For Paul the happy animal in him died. He could not waltz down life's way in selfish abandon now.

But God's Word, the Gospel, does not leave you a dead animal; it wants to make you a living prince. It wants you to face God and boldly call Him Father. It wants to replace for you the pleasures of the jungle with the joys of the palace.

You say, why did not God leave us alone to be animals? Why did He curse us with a conscience, and with this high assignment? Sixteen years ago King Edward of England abdicated his throne in order to marry a divorced commoner. It is questionable whether in the intervening years he has ever been able to enjoy the role of an abdicated prince, despite its pleasures and ease. And in his unhappy state perhaps he has cried in his soul, "Oh, why was I ever born for the palace?" Kierkegaard, in high irony, once said that mankind should gather together all the New Testaments in the world, carry them to a high

mountain, and cry out to God to take them
back to heaven, because the role it describes for
man is too cruelly high. The Gospel drives you
to this unhappy state, you who dare not quite
be a prince, because never again can you be a
romping animal.

It is at this point that we ought to pray for
the fullness of the Spirit!

Most of you, altogether too often, are trying to
be neither animals nor sons. And you think you
can do it, and still have the joy of the Holy Spirit
in your hearts. You live out on the edges somewhere, and come once in awhile, perhaps at a Sunday worship, to make a back entrance report to
the palace, a sort of polite call on the King, hoping
all the while that you will not really encounter
Him, but that someone will report to the King
that you were there. And out there on the fringes,
you handle your life pretty much as you please,
and intermittently pay a little voluntary tax, a
few cents or a few dollars, to the great King, a
gift so shamefully small that you hope the King
will never see the accounts. And when there is
a job to be done in the Kingdom, instead of tack-
ling it yourself with might and main, you always look out of the corner of your eye at the
other people and mentally calculate how little
can really be called your fair share. Or you hide
behind a wall of devilish humility and beg that
you are so little and incompetent that it is better

that you do not try at all. You want to do your
duty, but . . .

And then you wonder why your Christianity
is such an unhappy and unexciting affair!

You wretched and unhappy man. The Word of
God has broken through to you. You will always
be miserable trying again to be an unheeding sinner, a happy animal living wholly for self. There
is no other hope nor salvation for you—no house
of mirth—where life can be joy—than full within
the door of the palace. As long as you try to live
under the law, between good and evil, you will
always tend to calculate how little good you can
do and still be on God's side or how much evil
you can get by with and still escape His anger
and ultimate eviction. There is no escape from
this woeful discipleship but to let the Holy Spirit
usher you full into the blazing halls of the palace.

You need not be a hero to reach the palace,
battling your lonely way up some steep and
craggy ascent. You reach the palace by being *led*.
A divine Companion, the Holy Spirit, ushers you
upward and into its spacious halls. And He makes
sure that at no step along the way do you lose
sight of the Cross. For it is in the Christ of the
Cross that you have title to sonship with God.
With and in Christ you become His joint-heirs
to the Kingdom. The path, like His on earth, may
be beset with peril and pain, but with each step
the Holy Spirit bears witness with your spirit that

you are a child of God, and as such have every
right to the palace. And this growing assurance
in your heart will be the most sobering and exhilarating thing of all.

It is not easy to be a prince. A thousand voices
will woo you away from the high tasks of royalty.
You will be told that you are no more than the
accidental product of your heredity on the one
hand and your environment on the other. You
will be told that you are a most fortunate creature
because you are more complex than the chip-
munk, but that despite your oratorios and jet
planes you are an animal still. Nor will you be
offended, because it is really a great relief not to
have a kingdom on your shoulders.

While it is a relief to abdicate, your only joy
is to be found in the kingdom. You are doomed to
misery, and to spiritual death, outside. The native
element of the bird is the air; the native element
of the fish is the water; and, the native element for
man is the kingdom of God. To settle for less is to
die. You can never be mere man. You either are
led by the Spirit to be a child of God, and therefore more than mere man, or you turn away from
the Spirit and become an animal, something less
than mere man.

Let us cease our vain struggle against the Holy
Spirit. Let us give Him a chance to usher us full
into the palace and into the happy inheritance
our Savior-Brother is waiting to share with us.

Under the Big Tent

*And there was a cloud that overshad-
owed them: and a voice came out of
the cloud, saying, This is my beloved
Son: hear him. And suddenly, when they
had looked round about, they saw no
man any more, save Jesus only with
themselves.*   MARK 9:7-8

Man is rich in direct ratio to his sense of
wonder. If your affairs get so snarled up that you
cannot marvel at the color, texture, lines and
fragrance of a rose, you have lost much in life.
If you have become so grown-up that you cannot
stand under the night sky with your little girl,
and in real wonder, say with her . . .

> Twinkle, twinkle little star,
> How I wonder what you are,
> Up above the world so high
> Like a diamond in the sky.

. . . if you are too mature for this, you have for-
feited a vast empire of riches.

A few evenings ago the winds unleashed themselves in our city. If in that hour you were so

busy with the closing of windows or so fretful over falling branches that you missed the sheer exhilaration of nature's little display of power—in that moment of fret and fear you failed to cash in on one of your most precious possessions: the sense of wonder. I hope you have shared the imagery of William L. Stidger during some rainstorm:

> I saw God wash the world last night
> With His sweet shower on high;
> And then when morning came
> I saw Him hang it out to dry.
>
> He washed each tiny blade of grass,
> And every trembling tree;
> He flung His showers against the hills
> And swept the billowy sea.
>
> The white rose is a cleaner white;
> The red rose is more red
> Since God washed every fragrant face
> And put them all to bed.
>
> There's not a bird, there's not a bee,
> That wings along the way,
> But is a cleaner bird and bee
> Than it was yesterday.
>
> I saw God wash the world last night;
> Ah, would He had washed me
> As clean of all my dust and dirt
> As that old white birch tree!

However sensitive you may have become to the wonders of the world about you, there is a whole staggering world of wonder that the eye cannot see and the ear cannot hear. It unfolds only to men and women of daring Christian faith. It centers in one Jesus, and how He did wash mankind of all the dust and dirt of sin. The majestic splendor of the mountains, the endless reaches of the sky, the myriad sparkling of the stars cannot open the doors upon the wonder of God's love and grace. But there is a place—if in faith you will see and listen.

That place is the Cross of Calvary.

A ten year old girl went alone to the big circus. Her eye caught the long chain of tents. She entered the first, and at once was absorbed with strange and wondrous sights. All afternoon she wandered from one cage to another, from one spectacle to another; and at last, her head swimming with the sights she never before had seen, she followed the crowds home. It was years later before she realized that she had spent the whole afternoon among the animal tents and side shows, and had never gotten to the big tent at all.

The side shows of God's universe are the mountains and the oceans, the sky and the stars.

The big tent is where God Himself meets man, not in the wonders of His created nature, but in the incredible wonder of His own Son! Like the little girl, you may become so preoccupied with the visible world about you that you never once have had your breath taken away by the sheer grace of God in Jesus Christ.

Ushered into the big tent—into the presence of God as revealed in Christ and the Cross—you will encounter the strange sights and radical disclosures that "eye hath not seen." And if you stay there, under the big canvas, you will never be the same again.

There at the Cross, in the presence of Christ, you will see yourself as you have not seen before. Most of us see ourselves in the mirror of this world and our fellow associates. We struggle to stack up well by the standards of this world order. I work hard, I obey the laws, I am a faithful father and husband or a dutiful wife and mother, I develop skills in my craft or profession, I prosper economically, I may even give attention to culture and appreciate music and painting. I may explore the world of science and be a stalwart member of the community and church. Everything points up the fact that I am stacking up pretty well. And when I am gone, the whole world may say, "Well done, thou good and faithful citizen."

This record of my performance I bring into the presence of Christ—into the big tent. An utterly strange thing occurs! I feel uncomfortable. The smugness which the world's plaudits had conferred on me is gone. With Isaiah I am urged to cry, "Woe is me, for I am undone." Something has gone wrong; this earthly performance fails to conform to celestial standards. I am like an artist who comes to display his painting, and discovers in consternation that he should have painted a portrait instead of a landscape. I am like a student who reports for an examination after studying chemistry and discovers that the test is on Chaucer. I am like a statesman who had prepared for diplomatic service by the study of French, and learns that his appointment is to Finland. Within the big tent I discover that my earthly laurels have no relevance to the demands of God.

God demands holiness, purity of heart, nothing less. And while we are prepared to parade a creditable record of our works, we learn that God surveys the heart itself and that in every human heart, our own included, there is sin, impurity, envy and deep-seated selfishness. We had brought our pockets full of money with which to buy a nice cottage in the heavens only to discover that the sort of money we have has no exchange value in heaven. We had thought to have a cozy dinner with the great Judge, and we discover that the court has just pronounced upon us the verdict of guilt and the sentence of death. It is a fearful thing for a sinner to stand in the presence of the laws and judgments, the wrath, of the Almighty God.

If at this point I lose courage I may turn back to the side shows. If I do, I miss the supreme wonder. But if I stay, I will become aware of Someone at my side. It is my Brother, Jesus of Nazareth. If I fix my eyes on Him in faith, and see Him against a Cross, the breath-taking sweep of a new wonder will overtake me.

I am caught up in an old, old story. Told in countless ways, it is ever the same unbelievable gospel, or glad tidings. This Brother, anticipating my coming, has made ready for just such a moment and just such an emergency. Knowing that if I came at all, I would come without money and without price, He had laid in deposit for me in the real "coin of the realm" ample payment for my heavenly home. Knowing that I would be arrayed before the great court in the tattered rags of an inadequate and even irrelevant righteousness, over nineteen hundred years ago on a cross outside of Jerusalem He had died for me. His life of perfect holiness and His redeeming death were mine. He had lived and died for *me*.

There, in the big tent, all else fades away, and like Peter and James and John I see Jesus only. In this dreadful moment of examination and judgment I am saved by His grace alone. I begin to understand Paul, "For by grace are ye saved through faith; and that not of yourselves: it is the gift of God."

It is here that you confront the greatest wonder of the universe. Now you really stand under the big tent. Before you spreads the great redemptive act of God, and in the very center is a Cross. By contrast all the wonders of the arts and sciences pale into the shadows. You face not the majesty of mountains nor the mystery of the atom; you face the towering mystery of God's love for you. You are more important than mountains or forests, more important than the sun and moon and stars, because it was for *you* that the Lord of lords died.

As you stand before this wonder of wonders, something will start happening to you. Jesus says that what happens is so radical that it is nothing short of a "new birth." You do not try to measure up with God any more. You give up trying. But strangely, all fear is gone, because in faith you take the incredible gift of forgiveness and life offered by your Brother, Jesus Christ. Peace, a peace that is beyond any understanding, floods your soul.

A new urge, a new compulsion, fills your will. You stop scraping together your pennies of feeble works for a ticket to heaven, and you turn to pour out your life in thanksgiving to Him who has provided you a ticket. This you do not in order to be saved, but because by grace you already are saved. You live like a King's son not in order to become a King's son, but because you are a King's son. You stop quibbling over your credits, your fair share, your just dues—and turn to love as you have been loved, showing mercy as you have been given mercy. Having been washed clean in the eyes of God, you set about to clean up your life as a witness for the eyes of men. You no longer strut your assets, for you have no need further of boasting. You seek only to bring glory to Him by Whose grace alone you have salvation.

And your whole life through you will not cease to live in the unbelievable wonder of God's continuing love for you in Christ.

And the side shows? Strangely enough, as you are caught up in the life of Christ, every other offering in this amazing panorama of existence will take on an added glow and warmth.

First the Kingdom

> *But seek ye first the kingdom of God,*
> *and his righteousness; and all these*
> *things shall be added unto you. Take*
> *therefore no thought for the morrow:*
> *for the morrow shall take thought for*
> *the things of itself. Sufficient unto the*
> *day is the evil thereof.* MATTHEW 6:33-34

The most discussed play of the mid-century
has been T. S. Elliot's *The Cocktail Party.* Celia
goes off and becomes a missionary, and is crucified
on an anthill by the natives. Her companions, the
cocktail crowd, upon hearing it, begin to feel that
Celia's fate has made meaningful both her life
and death. They are mildly tormented to find
something to give their lives a meaning higher
than a round of parties.

What is it that points up your life? Are you
willing to work during the day, because when the
day is over there will be a party? What makes
you carry on over the dreary spots? Is it the money
you get at the end of the trail? For many a person
the only bright spots looming up ahead are a mug

of beer at the next stop, an unexpected letter in the next mail, or the visit of a friend. We are often like people driving unseeing through the mighty sequoia forests, missing altogether their beauty and majesty because the only thing occupying our minds is the menu for the next meal.

You can try tying life together with a menu or a fishing trip or a mint of money, but your life will be bleak and meaningless. You will need something stronger and more comprehensive to hold it together. Christ said that nothing short of the Kingdom of God would be needed to point it up with significance.

The Associated Press recently carried the winsomely tragic story of Private John J. McCormick, 28 year old paratrooper. From Korea he had written a letter to his two little girls, Joanne and Rose Marie. The letter arrived on Thursday, but that week on Monday their mother had received a grim telegram from the War Department informing them of his death. She read the letter to her girls:

"This is Daddy. I want you to listen and pay attention while Mommie reads this to you. Just try to make believe I was there, talking to you.

"I want you both to know that I'd be with you if I could, but there are bad men in the world, and if they were allowed to do what they wanted to do, little girls like you wouldn't be allowed to go to church on Sunday or be able to go to the school you wanted to.

"Maybe Daddy will have to go and help God up in

heaven, and if I do, I always want you to be good to Mommie. Do as she says, go to church, if your conscience tells you something is right, always stand up for it.

"I'll be in a hole fighting in a few days in a place called Korea, so I'm sending you all the love that's in my heart on this sheet of paper. Be good and God bless you.

"DADDY"

There are many daddies who will leave their girls and boys less than this "life and death" letter which Joanne and Rose Marie will always have. There are men whose children will be haunted by a fear that their daddies had never found anything worth dying for, and therefore nothing much worth living for either, except the dreary chase of money or pleasure or pride or comfort.

Man was made to live and die heroically. He was not made just to live and die, even if he could live without want and die without pain. It would be a tragedy, would it not, if we were to build a church to worship the living God and have our children use it to store grain. It is a greater tragedy when God creates a man to be the dwelling place of His Spirit and Kingdom, and we become mere containers for good food on the inside and surfaces for cosmetics and fabrics on the outside.

The glorious fact is that God has not doomed us to find meanings simply within the borders of this world's goods. He has established a Kingdom on earth. He has made a beachhead, and set up on

these far shores a matchless though invisible Kingdom. To do it, years ago He sent His only begotten Son to this earth, to live as we live, to
suffer as we suffer, to die as we die—and then to
rise again from the dead to a *new* and glorious
life. This Christ goes on before us, not as a field
marshal urging us to emulate him and do as he
has done, to fight and win; He goes on before
us with the simple invitation to enter into the
victory and the Kingdom which He already has
fully established. When we pray "Thy kingdom
come . . . ," we are to understand that the Kingdom has come indeed without our striving; we
pray only that the Kingdom might come to us,
or that we might enter into the Kingdom already
established for us. And within that Kingdom we
are promised life abundant. His invitation is
echoed in the words of Isaiah, "Ho, every one
that thirsteth, come ye to the waters, and he that
hath no money; come ye, buy, and eat; yea, come,
buy wine and milk without money and without
price."

If we come seeking, in the repentance and faith
which His Spirit works within us, we shall find
and be ushered in. And within this Kingdom new
vistas of meaning will unfold which we had never
suspected existed.

First we shall find that life gets wrapped up in
a *Person*. Instead of axioms or ideologies, hypoth-
eses or principles, life's interpretation centers in

the Person of Jesus Christ. This figure from the Sea of Galilee grows and grows until it fills the universe. Philosophy is swallowed up in a Personality. The wisest mind is caught up in the lilting refrain of the child, "Jesus loves me, this I know." A man discovers that if he shall have a faith strong enough to face death, and to meet life, it will have to be a simple child-like trust in this Overwhelming Person. It is not by chance that we have the picture of a Kingdom, with a King, instead of the picture of a republic or a democracy, with a fellowship. Nor is it by chance that this King is the Suffering Servant, the Savior come within our reach to give His life as our self-appointed Brother. With this King we can have fellowship, as with a friend or brother, and in that fellowship be wafted up to the heavenly plateaus.

Secondly, we are enabled to live meaningfully in a world where things do not seem to come out with fairy-book endings. Living within the Kingdom does not keep your automobile tires from puncturing, nor immunize you from mumps, nor stop death from stalking you. Christians have the normal supply of hard luck and the usual attacks of fear and anxiety. But they are not overcome by them, because they are buoyed up by an invisible Friend.

Life can be grim, despite the resources of God's Kingdom. A four year old boy wandered off from his home near the swamp and was lost. Hundreds joined in the search for him. His mother, at home, prayed ceaselessly that God would keep him from pain and bring him home alive. The third day they brought her his cold, wet, lifeless body. Life is like that.

A novelist describes two hostile families living on adjoining estates during the days of feudalism. One night the two rival noblemen went late into the forest to stalk one another to the death. In the darkness and storm, a tree fell and pinned them together under its trunk. Unable to extricate themselves, they lay there and talked it through and were reconciled. Toward morning they heard footfalls, and their hearts leaped with hope of rescue. Suddenly they both saw the blazing eyes of famished wolves. In the morning their families found their torn bodies. Life is like that.

Yesterday this church was filled with people who paid homage to the memories of a young father and mother, and who grieved over the two young sons orphaned, while five hundred miles away two men were left to go on with their drinking and homicidal driving relatively unharmed and unpunished. Life is like that.

Into the teeth of a world like that we fling the faith in a Kingdom which surmounts earth's tragedies with a strange and wondrous peace. Through the borders of this Kingdom the evils of life swirl with their toll of anguish and pain, but within these borders we are not dislodged and swept into despair. For we live in the strange assurance that God does all things well, and that in the final summation of things those who are within His borders will have all the loose ends gathered up and life gloriously complete. Moreover, in the very moment of the storm we are described in Paul's words to the Corinthians as people who ". . . dying, and behold we live; as sorrowful, yet always rejoicing; as having nothing, yet possessing all things."

And finally, though we have great confidence in this Kingdom's power to alter the life of this planet and make it more like the celestial order, our great trust rests in the certainty that our place in the Kingdom need never be forfeit. Though heaven and earth should pass away, the Word of promise which our Christ has given stands fast. We are His because on the Cross He died to give us title to Him. We are forgiven, redeemed and reconciled in His saving work alone. Luther's triumphant lines ring in every believer's heart:

> And should they, in the strife,
> Take kindred, goods and life . . .
> With us remains the Kingdom!

The Foundations
of Hope

> *Comfort ye, comfort ye my people,
> saith your God. Speak ye comfortably
> to Jerusalem, and cry unto her, that her
> warfare is accomplished, that her iniqui-
> ty is pardoned: for she hath received of
> the Lord's hand double for all her sins.*
> ISAIAH 40:1-2

Today I want to talk about hope. I need not be
an alarmist when I say that the world today is as
much without hope as it has been for many a
century. And if it is possible to recapture the
spirit of hope, we ought certainly to explore every
lead and every promise. Merely to admonish each
other with "Let's build up a little more hope"
we know will not do the trick. For hope is a tower
and a spire, and needs foundations. Before you
can build hope, you must build something else.

The architecture of God requires that we first
lay the firm footings of comfort and patience. The
apostle Paul has reminded us in Romans ". . .

that through patience and through comfort of the scriptures we might have hope." We start with comfort.

I do not know what you need most. Some of you need harsh talk. You are behaving badly and need some divine spanking. Others of you are making an earnest attempt to overcome temptation. You could stand some encouragement, even praise. Some of you, in sheer stupidity, are pursuing a mistaken course in life. You need instruction and guidance.

Whatever may be your peculiar needs, I venture to guess that there is not a person among you who could not stand some comfort. Most of you are not Sir Galahads, mounted on great, prancing steeds, eager to hear the charge "Forward!" Your spirits are not too high. More than likely, you are rheumatic riders on some spavined nags, with trembling hands and fearful hearts. You have deep wounds of the spirit to be healed, aching and tired muscles of the will to be massaged. Before God can talk the language of hope to you, He must fill your ears with His message of comfort. Before your spirits will be stirred with the challenge, "Be strong . . . acquit yourselves as men," your hearts will have to be comforted by the invitation, "Come unto me, all ye who labor and are heavy laden, and I will give you rest."

Precisely at this point is where the weight of

scriptures lies. The God of the Bible is not principally a field general pressing you on into the fight; much more often He is a field physician bending over your wounded spirits and your broken dreams. The kingdom of heaven is not pictured as an army regiment, with God the commander; the kingdom is rather a family, with God as a father. And do you recall from your own family or home what has characterized it more than any other quality? Is it not that there, more than in any other place in the world, you have found refuge and security and sympathy and comfort? Of course it was there that you learned the great lessons of right and wrong. There you may have been first inspired to noble living. But above all else, it was there that you could retreat from the indifference of the school, the shop or the office to find someone who cared, and who would give you comfort. I have liked these lines of the poet, because they so beautifully express that universal need of the heart.

> Backward, turn backward, O Time, in your flight,
> Make me a child again, just for tonight.
> Mother, come back from the echoless shore,
> Take me again to your heart, as of yore.
> Kiss from my forehead the furrows of care,
> Smooth the few silver threads out of my hair.
> Over my slumbers your loving watch keep.
> Rock me to sleep, Mother, rock me to sleep.

If the crowning tribute to our earthly homes is that there we have found understanding, and for-

giveness, and refuge, and comfort, it is even more
so with that home which is the kingdom of God.
Remember how often Christ prefaced His remarks
by such comforting words, "Let not your hearts
be troubled," "Be of good cheer," "Peace be with
you." And I cannot forget that magnificent cry
in the book of Isaiah, "Comfort ye, comfort ye, my
people, saith your God. Speak ye comfortingly to
Jerusalem. Tell her that her warfare is accomplished, her sins are forgiven, and she hath received double for all her debts." Read the Bible
from beginning to end, and the dominant message which God over and over again sends to His
people is the message of comfort.

And this comfort follows pretty well the three
pictures given in Isaiah. The first, "her warfare
is accomplished," we of the twentieth century can
certainly understand. When on V-J Day our head-
lines told us that the Great War was over, we were
released into profound thanksgiving and almost
frenzied jubilee. To hundreds of millions it was
the supreme news of comfort. In a deeper sense,
each of us is fighting a continuous battle against
forces that threaten constantly to overcome us.
The good intentions we send out on the field each
morning are cut down before evening by neglect
and indifference. The evil impulses we try to hold
at bay break through again and again to send us
back in retreat. And, look around you in the world
at large! We see little which could lead us to re-

joice that the forces of justice and mercy are winning the day against power and greed. In fact,
the postwar months, with their famine and disease,
their suspicions and hatreds, their greed and lust,
fill us with dread that the entire world is fast
losing its war against evil and disorder. In this
dark hour comes God's Word, that this inner and
profounder war really has been won. It has been
won, not by our feeble fighting, but by Someone
else. In Christ, the Lord of the Heavenly Armies,
God Himself has invaded this earth. On Golgotha's hill, He gained His bridgehead, and down
the centuries He has quietly and steadily been
occupying the realm of men. Satan and his princi-
palities have already, at Calvary, suffered a reeling
death blow. And we, if we will allow ourselves
to be recruited into the armies of Christ, we
already through faith are victors.

How goes the fight with you, my friend? Are
you letting your passions take you captive? Are
you giving up to bitterness or to boredom? Have
you let down the bars to let fears and hatreds and
suspicions invade the fortress of your soul? Are
you in full retreat? If you are, won't you make
one more stand? And this time won't you let the
overwhelming reserves of Christ's hosts come into
your heart to battle for you? Even Paul was in
rout. He knew that of himself he was through; he
could do nothing. But he had allowed a change
of strategy, and had discovered that he could

do all things through this Christ who would strengthen him. By being on the side of the Victor, he also became a victor.

The second picture in Isaiah's trilogy of comfort was that of forgiveness. "Tell her that her sins are forgiven." Like an overhanging cloud, a nameless sense of guilt blocks off the joyous sunshine of life for all mankind. A Christian missionary friend of mine told of asking a Chinese Buddhist priest, a friend of his, this question: "What, in your opinion, does Christianity have to offer that the Buddhist religion does not have?" After a long silence, the priest replied, "Christianity offers the forgiveness of sins." The apostle says, "If we say we have no sin, we lie, and the truth is not in us." We all have daily sins of thought and word and deed rising up to wall us off from peace. Only forgiveness, the forgiveness of God through Jesus the Savior, can remove the wall, and let the tidewaters of peace flood over our fretful souls.

The third parallel is the debtor and his debt. "Tell her that she has received double for all her debts." In ancient times a man who could not pay his debts suffered severe penalty. His lands were confiscated, his home was taken, and if that did not provide money enough, his wife and children could be sold into slavery, and he himself imprisoned. Think what it would mean to such a man if someone offered him, not alone enough to pay off his debts, but an equal additional sum as

capital stock with which to make a new start!
You and I are terribly in debt. Worse still, we
are embezzlers. Every day we take out of life more
than we put back in. No honest person would
have the audacity to claim that he by any amount
of honest effort had earned his health, his brain,
his skills, his family, his friends, his country, the
sunshine above him and the good earth beneath
him. However much property he may have
acquired, every bit of it he has by virtue of a
capital stock of health and ability and opportunity
which was given him. No matter how we figure,
we are insolvent beggars in the economy of life.
To us, the beggars, God gives assurance that in
Christ we are square with the universe; more
than that, we have in addition the inheritance
of heaven itself.

Now, that is the comfort. You are victors in
Christ, therefore rise up and walk in the dignity
and station of victors. Do not let passion and fear
and boredom push you around any more. Your
sins are forgiven. Stop grovelling in the remorse
of past wrongs and failures, square back your
shoulders and walk unafraid in the company of
men and God. Your debts have been paid, and
there is a huge account in life's bank on which
you can freely draw. Therefore, face tomorrow as
a man who is rich with a wealth that will never
pass away.

This, my friends, is the comfort of the scriptures, the comfort we have in the Christ who almost two thousand years ago came to this earth, to become our Lord and Savior. If we will rest on this foundation, there are no heights to which our hopes may not soar. Like beautiful spires, they will rise through the clouds of time to lose themselves in the endless reaches of the eternities.

Is God Fair?

> *If thou, Lord, shouldest mark iniquities,*
> *O Lord, who shall stand? But there is*
> *forgiveness with thee, that mayest be*
> *feared.* PSALM 130:3-4

Many a man has lost faith in God because the world seems topsy-turvy. The innocent suffer, the righteous are persecuted and the wicked prosper. And, if that is the sort of world which God has made and manages, how can a person put any faith in God?

You may be such a person. From the depths of your heart you may have cried, "Why cannot God at least be fair?" Why should a good son suffer because his father is in prison, and a renegade son be excused because his family is honorable? Why in war should a God-fearing soldier be killed and a drunken nobody be spared? Why in industry should a cunning and unscrupulous scoundrel become rich and his hard working, honest employee get cancer and die? Why in the life of nations should a brutal tyrant overrun a small peace-loving people and make them slaves? At every turn life seems unfair. And the cry is wrung from your lips, "Is God fair?"

When John Milton had stated the task of his great work, *Paradise Lost,* he prefaced his poem with this prayer:

> What in me is dark, illumine,
> What is low, raise and support,
> That to the height of this great argument
> I may assert eternal providence,
> And justify the ways of God to man.

Any person who tries to answer the question, "Is God fair?" will need to let God speak for Himself. This God has done in the Scriptures. If you are willing to hear the full message of the Bible, you will have an amazing answer to your question. You will discover that God is not only fair, but that He has gone far beyond the rule of justice in dealing with man. However unfair you may find the affairs of this earth, you will know that God Himself is much more than fair.

The first great truth of the Bible which you must fix in your faith is this: the pain and sorrow and death of the world are not God's doing. These are all intruders, thieves who came in through the back door against God's will. When God had completed His work of creation, crowning His work with the creation of man in His own image, the Bible declares that He beheld His work and, lo, it was all very good. Then sin came. Through the rebellion of Satan and the disobedience of man, the sinless and deathless state of man came to an end. God's perfect plan was violently disturbed. A horde of enemies descended upon man, hatred and murder, selfishness and vice, sickness and death.

However you explain the origin of evil, the Bible is clear in this, that you cannot lay it at the doorstep of God. You may have to leave the question of the beginnings of evil quite unanswered, but if you are willing to receive the full message of the Bible, like Job of old, you will absolve God from any blame. If you insist on blaming God, then I can see no comfort for you, unless you find some grim comfort in shaking your fist at God and heaping curses upon Him.

The only clean-cut manner of facing evil is for man to blame himself. Of course that does not mean that if you get cancer, or if a bomb blows up your home, you dismiss it by saying that God must be picking on you for some specific sin. But it does mean that the weight of mankind's ills falls on you as a member of a selfish and rebellious human family. Like Jeremiah of old, you repent for the sins of your people as if they are also your sins.

The second great truth which you should tuck away in your faith is that things work out with more justice than you think. The Lord knoweth the way of the righteous but the way of the ungodly shall perish. There are compensations, or pay-offs, for the upright which are not quickly evident, but are there, nonetheless. And, there are punishments for the wicked which no law court need administer—the uneasy conscience, the restless heart, the fear of discovery and reprisal, self-reproach, and the dread of overhanging judgment. "Day and night thy hand is heavy upon me," said David in his hour of wrong. And, he adds, "I would rather be a doorkeeper in the house of the Lord than to dwell in the tents of wickedness." The lot of the wicked in this sort of world is not a happy one. There is justice that works itself out relentlessly; and, if it is justice that you want in this universe, you have every good reason to believe that justice is here. A man gets what he has coming more often than at first glance you may think.

But faith in a just world is not very comforting, even for the best of men. Who among you would like to stand before God and ask for what you had coming, no more and no less? When, one day, you are summoned before His judgment seat, you will not strut your confident way forward and demand a fair deal. If God should be fair, and mark every iniquity, who could stand? Your hope will be that God will not be fair, that He will be much more than fair. With the Publican in the parable, you will cry, "Lord, be merciful to me, a sinner."

And that brings us to the third great truth, and by all odds the greatest, which the Bible urges you to believe. God is a God of mercy and compassion who in His only begotten Son has come to the world, not to judge but to save. This is the wondrous good news, the Gospel. Man who can only tremble in fear before a "fair" God, confronts the Savior God.

That God chose a cross and death for the salvation of man will always be beyond the reach of the mind of man. That He, too, should suffer, and that He, too, should die is the eternal mystery. Mystery though it be, it has had the strange power of filling this weary and frightened world with the only hope that it has known. The suffering was for you and me; the death was for you and for me. We cannot know why salvation had to come this way; it is enough for us to know that it has come this way. With an altogether strange gift, the gift of faith, we take hold of the truth, and it fills our life with a wondrous warmth and peace.

We do not want a fair God, after all, unless He also is a God of mercy. If Jesus had not walked across this stage of time, and enforced His claim to be the Son of God, the second Person in the Holy Trinity; if He had not lived and died as an atonement for our sins, and the sins of the whole world; and, if He had not the third day arisen from the dead as a triumphant confirmation of all His incredible promises—then this world of ours today would be no more than a lonely planet where lonely men would fight a brief and losing battle before swift death would end forever their fluttering hopes. But He did come, and He did die, and He did rise again.

This great truth about God enforces upon you and me a corollary for our own lives. Having been shown mercy, we in turn must be merciful. Having received such unmerited forgiveness, we are impelled to forgive. It is not enough for us to be just or fair. Living within the structure of governmental law, we must also live far beyond and above all law. We must live in the glorious liberty of the law of love.

It is only in the light of this sort of God, a merciful Savior, that the strange precepts of the Sermon on the Mount become intelligible. It is not fair that a man who strikes you on the right cheek should be allowed to strike you on the left also; nor that a man who sues you for your coat should be given your cloak also; nor that you should love your enemies and pray for them that despitefully use you. These are not the corollaries of justice; they are the sweep of mercy.

This old world is struggling desperately to create a framework for national and international justice. Only as mercy seasons justice, in Portia's words, will the structures of human justice produce equity and peace among men. For this is the nature of God and His Son, Jesus Christ.

Do You Believe
in God?

*Jesus answered and said unto them, This
is the work of God, that ye believe on
him whom he hath sent.* JOHN 6:29

Is a man godly because of what he believes or
because of what he does? To that question you
probably would disagree in reply. Some of you
would say that certainly what a man does is a more
sure measure of his godliness than what he believes. Others among you would vote for belief
being more basic and fundamental than behavior.

The crux of the matter lies in the meaning you
give to the word *believe.* The word does have
various shades and intensities of meaning. It may
be used in a harmless and indifferent sense, or it
may be made to carry the profoundest and revolutionary movement in life.

You say that you believe the world to be round
like a ball, or you may say that you believe the
world to be flat like a disc. In either event, all you

really say is that you accept one notion or another as the more likely explanation of the shape of our earth. Whether you believe one or the other, you will go on eating the same sort of meal, choosing the same sort of friends, loving or hating the same people, much as before. Your belief changes nothing for you. There are people who believe in God much in this way. Sure, they believe in God—so what? Does not every sensible person believe in God? But if someone should suggest that because they believe in God they ought to change their policies of business or labor, they would be quite shocked. A man certainly should be able to believe that Da Vinci painted the Last Supper, that God created the earth, and that Shakespeare wrote Hamlet without having to change his economics or his politics. Obviously, if that is what you put into the word *believe,* then it is not very important what you believe.

But the word does have a more dangerous aspect. Let us say that you believe Russia to be committed to a policy of world conquest. Because you believe this you may favor greater expenditure for arms. You vote for men who will budget more money for preparedness. This belief will shortly make a difference for you. Already you complain of your federal income tax, 79 per cent of which even now goes for military purposes. But your belief will increase your tax and take your money. It may even take your son when he finishes high

school, pluck him out from your home into some
program of universal military training. All this
may turn out to be most distressing, indeed; but
some such course of action is just what your belief
about Russia would inevitably do. It would reach
right back into your pocket for your money and
into your home for your son. This polite word
"believe" has turned out to have real teeth.

The word packs a bigger wallop still. Start
saying that you believe in your lover or beloved.
Because you believe in her, or him, you may marry
and tie up your life with someone for better or for
worse until death do you part. Now it becomes
supremely important what you believe; believing
in someone has altered your whole life.

Even so, we have not explored the ultimate
intensity of the word. To believe in God, in the
Christian sense, pushes the word to its highest
point and its widest reach. When the people asked
Jesus to describe for them what the works of God
were, He replied that to believe on Him would
be the work of God. By that He did not mean
merely to accept the notion that He was divine.
He meant that if we believed in Him we would
trust Him for all things more than we would
trust riches or friends. He meant that we would
fear Him more than we would fear cancer or war.
He meant that we would love Him more than we
would love mother or self. The man who really
believed in Christ would fear, love, and trust in

Him above all things. This is more than a little excursion of the mind; it is the total surrender to Jesus Christ as Savior, Friend and Lord.

Imagine an emigrant standing with his wife and child at the pier ready to embark to a foreign shore. In their bags are all their worldly goods, within their breasts are their plans and dreams. There they stand, all they possess and all their hopes, ready to walk across the plank to the ship. Suppose this man pauses to ponder, "Shall I entrust to this ship all that I am, all that I have, all that I hope to be and have? Shall I count on it to carry me and mine across the sea to the safety of a distant harbor?" It is a momentous choice and entails the sense of total risk. Some such thing is involved in faith. To believe in Jesus Christ means entrusting all things to Him, the course and direction of the voyage, the safety of the entire journey.

Just at this point we may miss the dangerous character of faith. The ship offers safe passage, but the ship has a fixed course. Many a man is willing to rely on God for safety, but he is unwilling to relinquish to God the direction of his course. To believe in Christ does mean salvation from eternal death and punishment, but it also means riding the route which is Christ's. We take up our cross, as He took His, and follow Him. His path becomes our path. As He loved us, we are to love one another.

If that is what believing in Christ really means, a person had better not be so glib about confessing his faith. It may take you out upon seas you had never thought to sail and thrust you into storms you had wanted to avoid. Like Him, you will have to become a servant of all. Like Him, you will have to forget about your rights and privileges and think primarily about your duties and responsibilities. Like Him, you will have to set yourself to doing the will of God, even if it plunges you into sufferings and takes you to the uttermost parts of the earth. If you really believe in Him, you may have to do what you had never expected to do with your dreams, your ambitions, your money, your very life. You will begin to understand, then, that what you believe is far more vital than what you do, simply because this kind of believing will determine everything you do.

We live our lives in the shallows, most of us. We are busy about many things and often forget to ask the simple but startling question, "Why are we busy?" Busy-ness is not enough. To do something simply to be doing something, leaves us in a great void. I have watched my little boy working long and carefully at building a house of blocks. When he is done, he may with one kick of his little foot scatter the house over the floor, only to start the repetitious process over again. Man's work on the earth seems often as juvenile as that. Civilizations built with long and laborious effort are scattered to bits by some weary and bored generation, only to have the historic process start the same cycle over again. This jittery twentieth century has done a pretty good job of kicking the blocks around into a new jumble. The reason for our strange behavior is not too difficult to see. Our work is tied to no faith, or belief, adequate to assure its survival.

To our bewildered generation Christ is eager to enforce the old truth, that basic to all work of enduring quality is *belief,* a faith of such commanding stature and of such comprehensive scope that in itself such faith becomes work. "This is the work of God, that ye believe on him whom he hath sent." Stop short of that and your work can be no more than a meaningless busy-ness. As such it will end in a tangled mass, ensnaring and choking the worker himself.

We face the Christ, the Christ of the Cross. Stop in your tracks, cease your darting here and there, and ponder the profound meaning of that Cross. There your sins are forgiven, there you are invited to a life of service to truth and justice and mercy. There heaven allows you a glimpse of life's meaning in its highest and widest dimensions. And if the Spirit of God will enable you even to whisper, ever so falteringly, the words, "I believe," you may begin walking in the newness of life.

Are Honesty and Decency Enough?

> *And Jesus said unto him, One thing thou lackest: go thy way, sell whatsoever thou hast, and give to the poor, and thou shalt have treasure in heaven: and come, take up the cross, and follow me.*
> MARK 10:21

"I'm not happy. I try my best to be decent. I don't lie or cheat or steal. I'm good to my wife and mother. I don't run around and get drunk. I've never been in jail. A lot of fellows play life free and loose, and sometimes I think they get on better than I. What's wrong? Why can't I be happy?"

That's about the way this young man talked to the Lord. "What must I do to inherit eternal life? I've observed the good rules of life from my youth up, but I haven't got that certain something on the inside which I know I should have." This young man was not fooling himself. He did not have it —this certain quality of life which gave richness and fullness to every passing hour—and he was frank to admit it. Perhaps he had overheard the Lord saying that He had come to give the life abundant, and had sensed something in the demeanor of Christ's followers which he was sure he himself did not have.

How many of you would be bold enough to stand up to the Lord and declare that you had found it? And if not, why not? Most of you have gone to church since childhood, and here in the church, through Word and Sacrament, it has been the Lord's good pleasure to give you the kingdom all along. Yet, like this young man, many of you have gone away wistful, a bit sad, never quite getting to the point where your spirit within has been aglow, your heart singing for joy, your feet striding out as if you had been crowned a prince.

This encounter of the Lord and the rich young ruler will give us a clue to our own troubles, and will shed light on the path we shall have to take to get it.

Implicit in this story are three levels of life, three sorts of people.

First, there are people who play life according to the rules of the game. They obey the laws, they observe the good customs, they do their fair share. They will say, and with some honesty, "All these things have I observed from my youth."

Secondly, there are people who play short of the rules. They violate law and good custom. They try to get by with the least possible effort. They are waste cargo, parasites in society. It would literally have been better had they not been born.

Third, there are people who play way out beyond the rules. They do not ask about what is their fair share; they see a good job to be done, and give themselves untiringly to see it done. And when they are through, they do not quibble about credit—they haven't time—they already are busy with some other good thing to be done.

For our purpose today, we can dismiss the man who plays the rules short. If in business he is unscrupulous and fraudulent, he may increase his income, but he is paying on the nose in innumerable hidden ways. His assets of human sympathy, self-respect, good conscience and deep peace are drained off at an alarming rate. If in his home he thinks he is deceiving his wife and friends and getting by with a loose life, he finds his better self and God dogging him around in dark places to torment him. A man who plays the rules short simply does not get by. If he seems to strut and dance his heedless way in safety, there is always the final moment of reckoning, when death clutches his collar and whirls him around to face the fearful accumulated judgment of his frauds.

It is the second fellow who intrigues us in this incident, the chap who plays the rules to the letter, the utterly fair person, the man who always carried his corner of the load. If there are ten bags of cement to be carried, he will uncomplainingly take his five if you carry your five. If there are eleven men on the team, he will take his one-eleventh share to win the game. He marries, and he will go fifty-fifty with his wife to make the home right. If the baby gets sick, he will sit up half the night if she will sit up the other half. If he belongs to a congregation, and the Lord asks them to send out a missionary, he sharpens his pencil and figures out the fraction that should be his fair share, and remits it in the next mail. You have known him, this careful, cautious, timid, frightened man of the rules.

And then he wonders why he does not care much for football, or why he is not very happy at home, or why religion does not excite him. He is not a shirker nor a cheater; he is just and fair. He obeys the laws, he plays by the rules—no less and no more—and lives out his days in utter misery, wondering why he never gets paid off with happiness.

And you have all seen some people of the third class. These are the men and women who play way out beyond the rules, who never pause to figure out what is their fair share. They do not ask, "What must I do to get by—what ought I do to be fair?" God and the high call of duty and the splendid commission to love combine to set before them a task. In sublime abandonment, they give themselves. They hardly have time to get very irked by the stragglers and grumblers. They may feel sorry for them, but they waste no energies in peevishness.

Frankly, I do not know what the world would do without these people who play beyond the rules. Even a commercial business will not survive unless in its organization there are men and women whose loyalty inspires them to give of their time and thought way beyond what is calculatingly fair. Our whole school system would be ineffective if we did not have teachers whose devotion for children did not make them lose themselves in their tasks. No home can be a real home of warmth and love on a fifty-fifty platform alone. And that which makes football a great game to watch is the fact that on the field are twenty-two men who have forgotten all about their one-eleventh share and are pouring out everything they've got because there are goalposts beckoning them at the end of the field.

Jesus was not peeved at this poor, rich fellow. Jesus, looking upon him, loved him. He felt a profound pity for him. So he shocked him to the roots, "Go, sell whatsoever thou hast, and give to the poor." Think what might have happened to him had he done it! What a story Cronin or Lloyd Douglas could have written about him! What an exciting and heaven-shaking time he could have had going around from hut to hovel brightening the lives of the sick and poor. Sure, his stocks and bonds would have steadily dwindled—but think what stupendous inner wealth would have been piling up for him day by day!

He did not do it. He went away sorrowful. He had his foot on the threshold of glory, and he stumbled back into the shadows of the neat, orderly and decent rules that had guided and robbed him from his youth.

Now, let us take a look at ourselves—a Christian congregation. We are Christ's community, His workshop, His own business establishment on the earth. However many other laudable enterprises engage your time and interest, the church alone is God's peculiar creation. As a church, a Christian community of people, we are an extension into this planet of the eternal kingdom. I am glad that in this congregation, as in others, there is the spectacle of men and women who play way out beyond the rules of fair and equitable shares of work and devotion. There are workers in the Sunday school and choirs who year after year give of their time, when they could say, "This year it is somebody else's turn." There is a magnificent corps who face the innumerable tasks in parish calling, in group activity, in kitchen, in programing and in giving, and who see only the goal-posts, and who long ago have left the neat rules far behind. But there are many who are missing it. Some of you are trying to hang on to a little equity on this thing called eternal life by an

occasional visit to a church service and a thought-
less bill thrown into an offering plate. And you
wonder why faith is such an elusive and unexciting thing! You cannot win playing the rules short.

The pity is that so many of you are playing in
splendid abandonment in your business, in your
work, in your homes, among your friends—but
you have not yet caught the sublime fun of playing that way with the enterprises of God, too. His
church, with its vast outreach of the Gospel in
missions, in education, in charities—all of which
is really the crowning glory of our free America—
should capture our imaginations at their highest
point. If your child is ill you would not hesitate
to spend all your savings, mortgage your home
and go to any lengths necessary to restore that
child to health. A world is ill, and you and I have
access to the great Physician. The Church offers
a vast program of bringing the patient to the
place of healing. What tragedy to be sitting with
sharpened pencils and calculating per capita
shares. The whole program of the church literally
shouts at you to throw this prim caution to the
winds, and to get out there where the sunshine
of His love can hit you and where the winds of
heavenly vision can play around that head of
yours.

This man of our text did not do it. And the
wistful question, "How may I inherit eternal life,"
remained unanswered for him.

What if he had sold all that he had and distributed it to the poor, as Jesus suggested? Would he then have found eternal life? Was it a problem of the amount he was willing to pay, like trying to buy a suit of clothes for $25.00 and being asked $75.00? The altogether disturbing and interesting fact is that he could have given away all and yet not have had eternal life.

When Nicodemus asked the same question, the Lord retorted, "You must be born again." Paul reminds us that the letter killeth but the spirit giveth life. Luke records the Lord as saying, "When you have done all, then say, we are unprofitable servants." The fact is that you cannot buy, earn, achieve nor attain eternal life. By grace are we saved, and not by works. Had Jesus succeeded in prevailing upon this rich, young man to sell all that he had, He then would have had to lead him on to the great secret. For, this struggling, striving, achieving, bargaining *you* must die, and a new *you* be born. Jesus was putting the young man on the path that would at last lead him to the great discovery that eternal life is always a gift, and not a purchase. It cannot be attained by observing the rules, nor by playing way out beyond the rules. It has been attained, once and for all time, by our Savior on a Cross; and thereafter it is His to bestow, as a gift.

To this great moment we bring nothing. We come with empty hands. Our finest performance will not avail. But the person who comes as a simple suppliant, a beggar, pleading only mercy —he, the repentant one, the trusting one—he receives in faith the strange and wondrous gift of forgiveness of sins and eternal life.

And having received, to play life's game even way out beyond the rules will seem for him but feeble thanks.

When You Look for
Your Place-Card

> *When thou art bidden of any man to*
> *a wedding, sit not down in the highest*
> *room; lest a more honourable man than*
> *thou be bidden of him; And he that*
> *bade thee and him come and say to thee,*
> *Give this man place. . . . For whosoever*
> *exalteth himself shall be abased; and he*
> *that humbleth himself shall be exalted.*
> LUKE 14:8ff

At the great dinner, where do you expect to find
your place-card? The Divine Host, the all-knowing
and all-seeing God, will check the list of guests and
arrange the seating. If by grace you are among
them, where will you start looking for your place?
Will you mutter to yourself that most likely your
name is up there at the head table, and edge up
to the center, or will you start looking down at
the foot somewhere?

If you start down at the foot, you will jostle
into some rather interesting people. Paul will be
elbowing his way to find the place for sinners of

whom he said he was the chief. Peter, the man who denied his Lord, will be down there overjoyed to find his name there at all. John the Baptist, who did not count himself worthy to unloose the sandals of his Host, will be there too. And Isaiah, the man who wept over his unclean lips!

Where at the table the Lord will have put your card only He knows. But it is tremendously revealing to know where you intend to start looking.

Nor is it likely that you will change your habits much at the last great dinner, the heavenly banquet of the bridegroom. If you have been blundering around the head tables your life through, you probably will be the same comic figure at the end too

If during your lifetime you have been sneering at your drunken neighbor, or if you have whispered about your stupid associates, or looked down your nose at the less prosperous, the less disciplined, the less intelligent and the less ambitious, you probably will strut your stupid social behavior right into heaven and be brought up with a most embarrassing jolt as you blush your way down toward the celestial kitchens to eat with the cooks.

The point is—over against God who knows all —the advantages you have really had in life and the shortcomings you have been able to cover up from the sight of men—over against Him, just how praiseworthy will be your achievements, just

how honorable, sincere, unselfish, kind, pure and
patient have been your motives? If He is to award
you precisely what you deserve, no more and no
less, where do you have a right to find your place
card?

This morning you have come into the presence
of God on the platform of confession. In the
prayers of the service you have said:

> Almighty God, we poor sinners confess unto Thee
> that we are by nature sinful and unclean,
> and that we have sinned against Thee
> by thought, word and deed.

And you did not go on to say, "But despite this
fact, we are better than many people who are
stupid, ignorant, dishonest, unreasonable and
mean, and therefore should merit Thy more dis-
tinguished treatment." That is not what you said.
You continued,

"We flee for refuge to Thine infinite mercy . . ."
You said in effect that if God by grace could give
you a place at the table at all, you would have
reason to praise Him forevermore.

Our whole secular life is pitted against this
sort of self-abasement which is the note of repentance. We are encouraged to a swagger and a
bravado which make all life a deception. We ride
along on slogans that advise men to put up a bold
front, that the race is to the strong, that God helps
him who helps himself, that clothes make the man,

that you are as important as you feel. Our whole modern life, so sensitive to the abortive art called salesmanship, is pitched to pretense and deception. The technique of success is first to deceive yourself into a sense of importance and self-confidence, and then to go on boldly pretending this importance to the world around you so that all men may be deceived into thinking you are just that important. Finally, we have the grand spectacle of fools fooling themselves and other fools. Lincoln cautioned men that you could fool some of the people all of the time and all of the people some of the time, but that you could not hope to fool all of the people all of the time. And there are two people you have an especially hard time fooling: yourself and God.

If you succeed in fooling yourself about your own importance, you become at once a comic and a psychopathic figure. And if you continue in the illusion that you are fooling God, you become a figure both tragic and damned.

You *are* important. You are a prince in God's own royal house. Of all the books in the world, the Bible makes the greatest case for your importance. God took personal delight in designing and manufacturing you. In Christ, He went to His death to redeem you. And, ceaselessly, through the Holy Spirit's work in Word and Sacrament, He is at work to remake you into a prince fit for celestial company.

But He has done, and is doing, the same for the pygmies in Africa, for the misguided and twisted minds of atheistic societies, for the demented patient in a padded cell and for the murderer in the prison. The fact that you have brains enough to attend college, health enough to work, personal charm to make friends, families to help and love you, and citizenship in a land of freedom and opportunity—these accidental circumstances of your life have no bearing on your place card at the table of God.

The only bearing these accidental variables of your life have is the compelling command to gratitude. If these fortunate aspects lead you to strut in pride instead of bowing your heart in humble thanksgiving, God would serve you better to take from you every lucky prop of your life, if thereby He could send you scurrying down to the foot of the table to shout a Hallelujah at finding your name there at all.

An ancient rubric in the confessional service before Holy Communion contains this cry, "Thou couldst with perfect justice condemn us for all eternity." If you really mean that, must you not go on to confess that God could with equal justice impose on you lesser misfortune? Must you not say, "God, Thou couldst with perfect justice burn down my house, strike me down with cancer, allow the death of my children, derange my mind, twist my body and torture my spirit"?

But are you going to take that sort of confession lying down? Are you not going to shake your fist in the face of God in protest and cry that it is unfair? Is it not highly unjust and unfair of God that your son lies buried in a Korean grave, that your crops are eaten away by rust, that your health collapses at the age of fifty, that hunger and pestilence and war ravage the earth?

I suspect that God deliberately invites your protest. He entertains more hope for a defiant atheist than for a whipped believer. The fact that He has created you an individual with the gift of freedom must imply that He wants you to stand up to Him. He does not want a weary collapse, a hopeless yielding. Job did not take his chastisement lying down; through long chapters in that memorable book he cries his protest to high heaven. Paul did not take his thorn in the flesh with quiescent fatalism; he battered the doors of heaven for release. But to Paul, as in fact to Job, God's answer was "My grace is sufficient for thee."

It is the answer He gives you, when life seems to deal you short. Instead of collapsing into bitterness and self-pity over injustice and adversity, you have opened for you a door of transforming wonder. If you lose your sight, His grace is yet sufficient. If your friends betray you and your dearest denounces you, if the skies fill with bursting bombs and the earth with rubble and debris, if

God's judgment seems to open the yawning mouth of hell to grasp your soul—the Word of God comes with the incredibly reassuring news, "My grace is sufficient for you."

Like Paul, protest if you like. But like Paul, let God lead you into His world of Grace. Until He has you there, He cannot go on to give you peace of heart, sweetness of spirit and courage of will. Until you are emptied of yourself and any claim upon the justice of God, He cannot convey to you Himself and the gifts of His grace.

It is at the foot of the Cross that you learn. At Calvary, where God Himself brought about your redemption, you are brought to repentance and trust. There you begin to comprehend the overwhelming wonder that in Him you do have a place at the table. It may be at the foot or at the head—what does it matter! What matters is that through Christ's redeeming death and resurrection your place-card is there.

This Freedom in Christ

> *Then said Jesus to those Jews which be-*
> *lieved on him, If ye continue in my*
> *word, then are ye my disciples indeed;*
> *and ye shall know the truth, and the*
> *truth shall make you free. . . . If the Son*
> *therefore shall make you free, ye shall*
> *be free indeed.*   JOHN 8:31ff

God wants to give man both freedom and righteousness, not freedom alone nor righteousness alone, but the two together. There are people who think of freedom as that state in which men do willy-nilly as they please, quite outside of any authority or standards. And there are men who conceive of righteousness as that state where man is restrained from doing what is wrong, even if it takes prison bars to achieve it. Freedom without righteousness becomes personal license and political anarchy; righteousness without freedom becomes personal bondage and political totalitarianism. One is as destructive as the other.

The clue to the nature of this dual gift lies in God Himself. What He is He wants us to be. Of all possible beings, God is surely the most free. In His freedom He could choose to create the universe, and should He so desire He could go on creating stars and planets without end. On the other hand, God is holy, righteous, and in all His free activity He never violates or trespasses upon His nature of holiness. His liberty is always exercised within the orbit of law.

If man is to share this dual character of God, he must first be reabsorbed into God. I say reabsorbed, because through the fall he became separated from God. In this separation he lost both freedom and righteousness. Apart from God, man's bravest attempts to recapture freedom and righteousness are illusion and only alienate him further into the blindness of pride.

How is man to be rejoined to God? In his blindness, man goes about to climb the ladder of discipline, good works, confident that if he succeeds in climbing high enough on the ladder he will at last reach the rung on which God stands awaiting him. If he slips a step or two, he reassures himself that if he tries, and tries again, at long last he most surely will succeed.

There is something gallant, and even something pedagogically necessary, in making this try. Without trying, it is not likely that a man will ever know personally the truth of that great triad of the Reformation: Grace alone, the Word alone, Faith alone. For how will a man really know that there is no other way to God than by the doorway of Grace if he has not earnestly tried the ladder of good works?

Luther surely gave himself a good workout on that ladder. As an Augustinian monk he not only submitted to the rigorous disciplines of his order, but he imposed on himself added self-denials in a fierce attempt to reach the favor of God. It was not until he had climbed and climbed and had succeeded only in reaching greater and greater despair that he was ready for the blazing alternative, Grace.

But many do not climb high enough to make Luther's discovery. Many settle down on the second or third rung of the ladder and live in the illusion that they have arrived. They become glued to a few trivial rules, and in observing them meticulously they settle back into a spiritual smugness, a priggish pride and a moral mediocrity. They have a form of godliness but have none of the spirit. They become a hideous caricature of freedom and righteousness. Moreover, it is almost impossible to dislodge them. Think how Jesus lashed out against this type, the Pharisees of His day. He told them that harlots and thieves had a better chance than they, for the very simple reason that these outcasts were not paralyzed by the illusion of righteousness. How can a man know the peril of the deep when he has never gone out into the water beyond his ankles, and when he lies down on the shoreline in stupid pretense that he is now a swimmer? Kierkegaard describes a Christian as swimming in seventy thousand fathoms of water.

Nor does a man better his position, nor the state of his world, by pressing up the ladder. The more intensely he pursues the disciplines of good works, the more susceptible he becomes to spiritual pride and to a harshness of morals that robs life of all its warmth and color. In Ibsen's *Brand,* the preacher senses the grim demands of the ladder—*alt eller intet*—all or nothing! And in his stern pursuit, he succeeds only in making a hell for his family, his parish and himself. In the end, when the avalanche is about to engulf him, he hears from the thunder of the rolling rocks the message of God, "Deus Caritas"—God is grace! We reach the state of freedom and righteousness, salvation, or life with God, only through grace, the grace that is in Christ Jesus.

Somewhere, somehow, God must shatter into bits all our boasted pretense to be deserving of Him, our confidence in climbing, if He is to usher us up to the doorway of grace.

For our hope must be in Christ and His performance for us, not in ourselves and our performance, if we are to have peace. At the foot of His Cross, where the Holy Spirit opens our eyes to our own deep sinfulness and incompetence and to the wondrous significance of His redeeming death, we discover the sheer comprehensiveness of grace. We are justified by grace alone. He won us, we did not win Him; He chose us, we did not choose Him; He saved us, we did not save ourselves. In Him we are again at one with God. Gone forever is the ladder; we are done with it. It did not bring us to God; it cannot keep us with God. We are both brought and kept by grace.

We owe allegiance now to but One, we heed but One Voice. And this One, in Whom we live and move and have our being, lives within us. We share His life, and out of His life there wells up within us the one law that is His very nature, the law of Love.

It is at this point that other voices make their subtile bid to re-engage us under false authority, and to annul our freedom. We are to obey God rather than man. But man, in one form or another, has variously tried to pose as the voice of God. In this dread moment, we need to remember the second of the Reformation triad: the Word alone.

Historically, this subtile and satanic seduction of the free man in Christ has taken three forms. The kings of the middle ages laid claim to the divine right to be the voice of God. If the man of God wished to know and do the will of God, let him obey his king! A second form has been the ecclesiastical lure. If a man of God wished to do the will of God, let him give uncritical obedience to the prelate—pope, pastor, priest, or church council. It was against this peril that the Reformation levelled its crushing blow, and from which it emancipated again the free man in Christ. The third and current form for us is the fiction that the voice of the people is the voice of God. Not the king, nor the prelate, but the cumulative wisdom of the majority of the people will yield the voice of God. For us in the U. S. A. who exalt the *demos*, the people, this peril to the freedom of the individual, the man of God, may be more devastating than all. The free man in Christ cannot pass the buck, cannot delegate his conscience, to king or pastor or people. He is under the awesome and splendid obligation to stand alone before his Lord and Savior, and guided by His Word alone, make the choices that the myriad of life's circumstances forces upon him. He is aided by the fact that he is of a great fellowship, the communion of saints, but until the end his freedom impels him to be a lonely figure before the will of his Lord. If he pursues his way in and by the Word of his God, in that truth he shall indeed be free.

His whole life will be held fast and empowered by a totally novel quality which life in Christ gives him, the quality of faith, the third of the great triad: Faith alone. This triad, like a geometric triangle, must have all three of these towering truths to have any one of them meaningful. With-

out faith, Christ's work in justifying us before
God would be inaccessible to us. His Grace is
ours by and in faith. Without faith, our wills
would remain dead and impotent for any good
work. Our lives can be pleasing in His sight only
as they are the fruits of faith. Without faith, our
minds would wrestle in vain for the answers to
the deep questions of existence. Wisdom and
truth are ours as we see with the eyes of faith.
Without faith, our hearts would writhe in fear
and dread; with faith they rest back into the
fathomless love and mercy of God.

We are a people of the Reformation heritage.
We trace our paths back to Luther, to be sure,
and to St. Augustine and to St. Paul. But we
have our freedom not from any man or men.
Our freedom is from Him who assured us that if
we would continue in His Word we should be
His disciples, as His disciples we should know
the truth that would make us free, and that because, He, the Savior-Lord had made us free,
we should be free indeed.

Saints and Salt and Light

Ye are the salt of the earth: but if the salt have lost its savour, wherewith shall it be salted? it is thenceforth good for nothing, but to be cast out, and to be trodden under foot of men. Ye are the light of the world. A city that is set on an hill cannot be hid. Neither do men light a candle, and put it under a bushel, but on a candlestick; and it giveth light unto all that are in the house. Let your light so shine before men, that they may see your good works, and glorify your Father which is in heaven.
MATTHEW 5:13-16

Most people shudder at the thought of being saints. If someone should slap you on the back and say, "You old sinner, you!" you would consider yourself complimented. If, on the other hand, someone should say, "So you're one of those saints, are you?" you would probably feel incensed enough to punch his nose.

In the safety of these church walls you have

this morning confessed your hope that you might
be a saint, and be a part of the royal company
called "the communion of saints." But you would
very likely bristle up if this afternoon someone
should address you as one of those saints from
First Lutheran Church.

For most people the word "saint" has gotten an
altogether wrong meaning. In fact, the definition
is normally given in precise reverse from what
the word ought to mean. And the average church
goer is as misguided as anyone.

You imagine Saint Peter to be a naive, old
fisherman who in his youth might have been a
great fullback if he would not have had to learn
more than about two plays a season. You regard
Saint Paul as a weasel-like fellow who, though
rather sharp, went overboard on a vision he had
on the road from Jerusalem to Damascus and
never after quite recovered his common sense.
You imagine Saint John to be a mild dreamer
who babbled about love and ended his days writing some unintelligible drivel called *Revelation*.
And you have heard about Saint Francis who
got a quirk and gave away his wealth and princely
station to become a voluntary beggar writing
sweet things about birds and angels.

Thus you emerge with your notion of what
makes a saint. And you have the image of a person
not ambitious enough to make a dollar, not pas-
sionate enough to lust after a woman, nor

courageous enough to get angry, nor healthy enough to go hunting. You picture him, a pale anemic, going about singing in a thin tenor,

> Thou art the potter,
> I am the clay.

> O to be nothing, nothing,
> Only to lie at His feet.

Now, is not that very nearly the picture that you have had? Robert Ingersoll once declared that occasionally a well-meaning person, often an elderly woman, sees a young man not quite sick enough to die nor healthy enough to be wicked, and she concludes that he would make a fine, orthodox minister. Not quite sick enough to die nor healthy enough to be wicked—that describes the "saint" for many people.

Have you ever imagined a saint knocking out Joe Louis in the ring, or commanding a million men in war, or amassing a million dollars in oil or wheat, or being the whip in congress, or standing up unflinchingly to the threat of death in a concentration camp, or spanning the seven seas for a cause?

If you have not, why haven't you?

Just what is a saint? Simply stated and most important, he is a person whom Jesus has saved and taken to Himself. To be sure, that is not the picture of a hero standing up to God or battling Him on even terms in a boxer's ring. You are a

saint not because you have held your own with
God. In repentance and faith, you have capitulated to Him. But from that point on you do not
go on capitulating. You, the saint, are surren-
dered to God; but you do not go on surrendering
to anyone but God.

God is the potter, and you are the clay. But
God is not moulding you into a fragile vase to
contain fragile flowers. He is out to make you
into a sort of potter. He, the great Creator, is in-
tent on making you into a wondrous, creative
being. You are to be like God. You are to run
around in God's gang, in the company of the
saints, angels and archangels, forevermore.

Here you stumble, too. Your picture of angels
is askew. You see your chubby five-year-old
daughter tripping around at a Sunday school
program with tissue paper wings, and who wants
to spend his days in a kindergarten! The fact is
that the Scriptures use the masculine gender when
referring to angels, and names like Gabriel,
Michael and Raphael do not evoke the imagery
of lace and tissue paper. We would be more true
to the Bible's imagery if at our next Christmas
program we would marshall the fathers as angels.
And, if any father wishes to volunteer for the
role, particularly if he weighs over two hundred
pounds, we will be glad to enter him in the cast.

Saints are steel, not straw. Some years ago I
visited a town the day after a tornado had laid it

waste, and among the many queer phenomena of the storm I saw a stalk of straw driven through a telephone pole, as steel. When God makes you over into a saint, He changes you from straw to steel. Saint John, in *Revelation,* refers to the saints as pillars, with footings on the rock, upon which the entire structure of the building must rest. In our text today Jesus calls them the salt of the earth, that which keeps the whole from rotting away. In His day in Palestine good salt was absolutely essential to keep the fish and meat from spoiling. He calls the saints the light of the world. If some night in this darkened church one single candle should be lighted and suspended in the center of this space, every nook and corner of this large church would be touched by the play of its light and shadow. To be a saint is to be like that!

The tragedy, says Christ, is that the salt may lose its savor and the light may be hidden. If the saints should become indistinguishable from the mass, then like savorless salt it would utterly fail its role and task. If you and I, as Christians, talk like the rest, in slander, gossip and blasphemy; if we live like the rest, showing concern only for those we like, voting only for the candidates who will pad our interests, giving only when we have to give to be respectable—then we have become salt without savor, quite useless for both God and man.

And how many of us who bear the name Christian, the highest label in earth, fail woefully to be marked as Christians? Our lights are under a bushel, and under the bushel the oxygen supply quickly runs out. In your conversation at the shop or in the office, within ten minutes you will reveal whether you are of the Republican party, whether you favor price supports or are against them, whether you drive a Buick or a Ford. And from some button in your lapel or some ring on your finger you flaunt your membership in a lodge, a fraternity or club. But some of you have worked for years in some office and have neither by word nor deed given your fellows any inkling that you are an earnest Christian.

To be sure, there is something abhorrent about a person who goes prattling about things that are precious enough to be kept somewhat in private, like the love you have for your wife. But most of us stand indicted not for declaring our faith enough, but for failing to let our lights shine. How many of you would hesitate in telling your friends how much money you give to your church because you fear to be boastful, rather than because you would be ashamed of its trifling amount?

You are the loved ones of God. In Christ He has redeemed you to be His own. You are to be His ambassadors, to speak His Word and to witness to His life. In our country you need not be an underground movement, a secret society of the catacombs. We are to be the humble, courageous army of God on the open field.

And we are an army. There are over seven hundred million people who bear His name on the earth. If there were only seven hundred, or seven, we would still be in the mightiest army in heaven and earth. For as Christians we are of the communion of saints, in the company of God and the angels; and if you were the only saint on earth, you would still be the point of greatest power on the earth. If on the island of Okinawa there were only seven Americans among the half million inhabitants, these seven would still represent the mightiest nation on earth, despite their few numbers. You have the strength and glory of God's great company, not because you are among the millions who belong to the organized church but if and because you have Christ dwelling in you through faith. One grain of salt still fresh or one light not under a bushel has more power than a whole barrel of flavorless salt or a whole city of lights that are hidden.

The striking power of the church of Jesus Christ is its living, vibrant faith and its flaming, open witness. If we are true saints, we will talk and live in such a way that the world will find in us a clue to Father and His power, and will be led to Him.